ENGLISH LITERATURE
BETWEEN THE WARS

BY THE SAME AUTHOR

Criticism and Biography

Tradition and Romanticism
English Poetry in the Later Nineteenth Century
A Short History of English Literature
Keats
The Poetry of William Morris

Travel

Encounters

Fiction

In Search of Stephen Vane
The Shop on the King's Road

ENGLISH LITERATURE
BETWEEN THE WARS

by

B. IFOR EVANS

METHUEN & CO. LTD. LONDON
36 Essex Street, Strand, W.C.2

First Published . March 4th 1948
Second Edition . July 1949
Third Edition . 1951

66774

CATALOGUE NO. 3228/U

PRINTED IN GREAT BRITAIN

TO
SIR FREDERICK MAURICE

PREFACE

A part of this volume was delivered as lectures at the University College at Bangor, under the Ballard Mathews Foundation.

B.I.E.

CONTENTS

CHAPTER I

THE GENERAL BACKGROUND

THE practice by which names, whose immediate application lies in history and politics, are employed to divide the arts into periods is open to a number of obvious objections. At the same time it can be agreed that the years between the war of 1914-18 and the war which began in 1939 constitute not only a separate age in literature but mark a new era in which the whole mind of man and his conception of his destiny have changed in a fundamental way. The test of genius within the period is largely the degree to which a writer has been able to convey into imaginative forms an awareness of how profound these changes have been. In looking back over these decades one sees so much work of obvious technical agility and alertness, which yet somehow falls flat when the ultimate computation is made. The missing quality is often difficult to discover, but it lies always in some failure to recognize that human life is passing through a great tragic period. For the second, third and fourth decades of this century have seen not only destruction, human and material, unparalleled in recorded history, but the mind itself has revealed a capacity for evil of which it was previously unaware.

In England the shock of this change was all the more severe, as the opening years of the century, particularly from 1906 to 1914, had been full of hope. They formed a period of economic prosperity, of expanding opportunity, and in many minds of an increased faith in humanity and in its capacity for progress. England was not without self-criticism in those years, but it was allied to a generous belief that the ' Island Pharisees ' were

capable of improvement, that social injustice could be eliminated by a process of gradualism, and that imperialism could
in time and without violence be assimilated to democratic
ideals. Above all it was to be a world where man would have
increasing opportunities of exercising his attainments to the
full. It may well be that such impressions were illusory, and
that any portrait of society as a whole would have yielded large
ranges of suffering, depression and disillusionment. But the
vocal elements, which were mainly of a middle class, as yet not
deprived of its confidence, gave expression to a conviction of
the desirability of the world in which it lived and of its faith
in a general capacity for improvement.

Throughout the first decade of the twentieth century there
had been a literature of social criticism of which H. G. Wells,
G. B. Shaw, and John Galsworthy were the main exponents.
They were all anxious to reform the world, but they did not
question the ultimate possibility of reform, nor postulate the
inadequacy of man as an instrument for the good life. Nor
did they have any conception of a possible disruption of civilization. Wells and Shaw sometimes questioned the inevitability
of progress, but never during this earlier period did they
explore this idea with any seriousness. Nor were any of them
interested profoundly in the nature of the human mind itself.
Shaw's characters were too frequently automata whom he hired
to deliver his own brilliant speeches. Wells, along with the
well-ordered asylums which he planned for humanity in his
theoretical volumes, did portray characters such as Mr. Kipps
and Mr. Polly, poignant, irrational, and inconsequent. But he
never allowed them to walk into the new Utopias which he
was erecting with another part of his mind, and he never
admitted even to himself, that they were the instruments from
which life had to be made. One of the extraordinary phenomena is that both Wells and Shaw lived on throughout the
inter-war period and kept themselves aware of the changing
shape of the times.

Galsworthy had obviously a less cosmic imagination, and he is far more often deluded by the form of things as they are than was either Shaw or Wells. He possessed a considerable talent in portraying types, and his Forsytes will be long remembered, but ultimately he was attached to the upper middle-class society which in a mild and good-mannered way he was satirizing. If he ever looked at the ultimate tragedy, cruelty, and ecstasy that lie in the nature of man he never brought the knowledge he had acquired back to the service of his imagination. A sentimental foundation governs the pseudo-objectivity with which he surveys the world. The best of his work was over with the publication of the complete *Forsyte Saga* in 1922. *The White Monkey* (1924) and the later novels in which he recorded the inter-war scene were superficial and sometimes even meretricious. They were surface reports of a limited validity, and certainly they were devoid of any comprehensive vision. Whatever may be the condemnation of the younger critics, *The Forsyte Saga* will hold a place not so far below that of Trollope among the chronicles of English life, but the thinness and falsity of the later work is already apparent.

In the period after 1918 this concentration on social criticism modifies as can be seen most clearly in the novel. The novelist may still remain the critic of society, and indeed D. H. Lawrence is far more violent and ruthless in such criticism than Galsworthy. Lawrence in his bitter attack on Galsworthy seems fully conscious of the difference in their approach. For beyond the social preoccupations the novelist returns to the study of the nature of man. That exploration of the individual personality is ultimately the unifying element in work as different as that of E. M. Forster, James Joyce, D. H. Lawrence and Virginia Woolf. As is suggested later in this chapter, the novelist was assisted by psychological methods which an older generation had never employed in such a self-conscious way, and the very emphasis in this age on psycho-analysis led him to the more profound study of the human personality. But beyond this, the war of 1914-18 had stirred a vision, never as yet forgotten, of cruelty and evil in man's nature which would have proved fantastic and inconceivable in the first decade of the century.

This led, however indirectly, to a new and creative attempt among the more original writers to explore the nature of man's mind. During the earlier years of the century most men had still believed in progress, even when they denied its existence, and they believed in the permanence of things as they are, even when theoretically they were on the side of change. They indulged in the benefits of a bourgeois civilization, even when in their writings they had condemned its very presence. Now in this inter-war period the vision, though never complete, is more profound. Man waits, often frustrated, at the door to a new era. He waits unhopefully, for the immediate prospect seems to be war and the ultimate conclusions are threatening and uncertain.

Even as early as the nineteenth century the study of evolution had led some minds to question, either temporarily or in a permanent way, the atmosphere of optimism with which they were surrounded. Tennyson had been thus, for a time, reduced to scepticism, as is recorded in *In Memoriam*, but he had found release in a confident reaffirmation of the Christian faith. Meredith, beginning with the same dilemma, had discovered a positive belief, largely of his own invention, based on his study of man's relation to Earth. Thomas Hardy (1840-1928) was not so easily consoled. He took a long, firm, cold look at life, and though his heart was full of pity for human creatures, he would not permit this to disguise from himself a fear, powerful enough to be a creative impulse, that man may be the helpless and tortured puppet of a blind destiny.

Though the modern writer has other evidence, more immediate and terrifying for assessing the influences which disrupt civilization, the quality of Hardy's tragic vision gains a close identity with modern circumstances. Of nineteenth-century writers he is the least rendered old-fashioned and inadequate as he moves forward into the twentieth century. Nothing that has happened in between seems to diminish his insight into the relentless nature of the destiny that governs human life. From the controversies which have affected literature in the inter-war period he was fortunately exempt. In the year in which *The Well Beloved* was published, and the year after *Jude the Obscure* had aroused such senseless and vulgar attacks, he had withdrawn from the practice of fiction. The loss was considerable, but in compensation Hardy had found himself in the new century as a poet. Already as early as 1898 he had published *Wessex Poems and Other Verses*, and the first decade of the present century was marked by his epic drama of *The Dynasts* (1903, 1906 and 1908).

Among later volumes were *Late Lyrics and Earlier* (1922), *Human Shows*, *Far Phantasies*, *Songs and Trifles* (1925), and *Winter Words* (1928). The novelist whom the abuse and blunted vision of the public had lost in the 'nineties thus developed into a considerable twentieth-century poet. Younger writers and critics have been sufficiently impressed by his massive achievement to exempt him from the attacks which they directed at many of his contemporaries. Further, he has been exceptionally well served by those who have written of his work, Lionel Johnson, Lascelles Abercrombie, and Lord David Cecil.

He was secure because he had hoped little from his age and had no illusions about life itself. At times he failed to give this negative approach the force of creative vision, and there are occasions in the later volumes when he sinks into despondency. Even in such moods he maintains a qualifying serenity, an open acceptance of destiny, and a consistent avoidance of self-pity, which remains as ever the meanest of the emotions. Further, he had freed his verses from the melodious language of the romantics, without ever disparaging their achievement.

Naturally, almost innocently, he had discovered his own manner, and unlike some in the following generation he had never found it necessary to proclaim his innovation by parading his own cleverness or superiority. His vocabulary was individual, avoiding all that was decorative and rhetorical. While it has little in common with the wit and the complex imagery of modern poetry, it was accepted along with its themes, as marking a conscious departure from the easy and melodious felicities of the romantics.

Though what is most memorable in his poetry is confined to a small number of lyrics, and to *The Dynasts*, little in it loses its quality with changes of fashion. In September 1914, he wrote one of the most memorable of war lyrics :

> What of the faith and fire within us
> Men who march away
> Ere the barn-cocks say
> Night is growing gray,
> Leaving all that here can win us;
> What of the faith and fire within us
> Men who march away?

The lines are untouched by time. They might equally well stand for September 1939, or for any month when man again may hear that impelling call to conflict, which seems incredible until it actually occurs.

For Hardy, except in a few uncertain moments when he dallied with the possibility of the union between reason and religion, the period between the two wars marked the beginning of a new barbarism. It was this firm acceptance of life's tragedy that separated him from the optimism of many in his own generation, and endowing him with a certain prophetic quality united him with the generation which was to follow. So in the preface to *Late Lyrics and Earlier* he writes : ' Whether owing to the barbarizing of taste in the younger minds by the dark madness of the late war, the unabashed cultivation of selfishness in all classes, the plethoric growth of knowledge with the stunting of wisdom, a degrading thirst after outrageous stimulation (to quote Wordsworth), or from any other cause, we seem threatened with a new Dark Age.'

In a minor way, A. E. Housman had maintained the same aloofness from his own generation and consequently possessed strong survival value. *A Shropshire Lad* had been published as early as 1896. It was not until 1922 that this was followed by *Last Poems*. Though as a whole it had little to add poetically to *A Shropshire Lad*, it did contain *Upon an Army of Mercenaries*, the epitaph in eight lines on the men who fell in the war of 1914-18 which seems by its unemphatic brevity, its classical reserve and yet comprehensive vision to say something of man's fate in the modern world which the years cannot destroy. Housman's influence and popularity have been very considerable, for his lyrics proved to be singable and have attracted English composers such as Vaughan Williams. The economy and the beauty of their phrasing gave effects which were original, though one might detect traces of Stevenson, Kipling and many other English writers, and there are clear marks of Latinity. The emphasis in Housman's lyrics on tragedy seems a device, or a mood, sometimes not wholly detached from morbidity, and lacks that cosmic vision which Hardy in all his major work possessed. He was remembered best for the earlier volume for, apart from one or two pieces, the *Last Poems* had added little that was new.

In an age when poets wrote much of themselves he had retained an objective and dramatic detachment. Further, there was some strange piquancy that this professor of Latin, this acrid commentator on his rivals in classical editorship, should preserve such an insight into the tragedy of life, and should possess some sardonic enjoyment of the irony that often underlay even the tragedy itself. Though Housman cultivated a remoteness from his own age he was fully aware of what was happening in modern poetry and criticism. His lecture on

The Name and Nature of Poetry was a challenge to the criticism which made extravagant claims that the study of poetry would benefit by logical and scientific methods. Delivered in Cambridge, it seemed expressly directed at a school of criticism which, while brilliant and serious, was in danger of pretentiousness, and of overbold claims for its own methods. Housman's reflections in the lecture also suggest an appropriate modesty in the artist, as if he were deliberately opposing those who assumed for the arts a larger place in society and in human thought than they could rightly claim. The whole text is full of biblical references, and a strange Old Testament fervour possesses it.

While in their several ways Hardy and Housman may anticipate more modern moods, they belong to a small minority. The majority of English writers in the period before 1914, and indeed in the first years of that war, had no premonition of an impending disaster. For that very reason their successors have turned upon them with a criticism and satire that seem often both unwarranted and unjust. From 1911 to 1922 a series of 'Georgian' anthologies had been published under the editorship of 'E.M.' (later Sir Edward Marsh). These presented a great variety of mood, but dominant among them was a sense of enjoyment of the English countryside, which was part of a welcoming appreciation of life itself. There was in some of this poetry a dangerous type of surface optimism which seemed deliberately to avoid all the harder things in life. The poets had the appearance of making things too easy for themselves and for their readers. They came to have the reputation of being week-end nature poets who indulged in their temporary pleasures without regard to the more profound problems of their time. They seemed to avoid the great urban centres, as Tennyson's knights in the *Idylls of the King* had seemed to move about nineteenth-century England, deliberately avoiding the industrial towns.

Nor were the values explored by a typical poet such as John

Drinkwater any more exacting than the emotions aroused by his descriptions of the natural background. Poetry had lost a dimension in much of this anthology verse. Consequently when the world later presented a harsher outline the attack against all this warm confidence and cheerfulness concentrated in denigration of the 'Georgian' School. The poets of the later generation who conducted the assault did so with great fury and technical brilliance. It was inevitable that such an attack should take place, and while some critics, such as Middleton Murry, attempted a balanced view of the limitations of this group of 'Georgians', the main assault was one of unreasoning violence, very similar to that which an earlier generation had conducted against the Victorians.

While all this can be admitted to have been inevitable, the time has come when the work of these writers should be more soberly assessed and the elements of injustice in the criticism removed. In common honesty certain things should be remembered. The war of 1914-18 took such a very heavy toll of the manhood of the country that a large number of young poets were removed before they reached maturity. Those anthologies were largely selections from the works of young poets, and were marked by Sir Edward Marsh's skill in detecting the earliest signs of talent. Secondly, many of the poets who began in those 'Georgian' anthologies must be exempted from any general condemnation, because their work will not fit into the descriptions which their detractors have framed. So numerous, indeed, are those who do not deserve the strictures lodged against this 'Georgian' type of poetry that they would make a respectable register for any decade, Walter de la Mare, D. H. Lawrence, W. H. Davies, Lascelles Abercrombie, Laurence Binyon, and others.

Of these Walter de la Mare, born in 1873, remained a poetical force throughout the inter-war period and, partly because he was a man of lovable character but mainly because of his poetry, he retained a wide respect. Older readers continued to

admire him and the young respected him. In a volume such
as *The Veil* (1921), he seemed to yield to realism, and there is
the same restlessness and distrust of the beauty which had been
traditional throughout his early work in his novel the *Memoirs
of a Midget* (1921). Happily the earlier moods returned in such
volumes as *The Fleeting and Other Poems*. They remain even
as late as 1945 in *The Burning Glass*. Magic, beauty, and childhood are here caught into a delicate web of verse, and their
presentation is strengthened by one's consciousness that the
mind perceiving them has wisdom and is aware of the great
realities of life and death.

D. H. Lawrence was to be remembered mainly as a novelist,
but in verse too he matured and strengthened in the period
between the wars. Particularly in *Look We Have Come
Through* (1917), he explored the deepest and most intimate
elements in his experience. Both in thought and in metrical
forms he showed experiment and independence. Much of
Laurence Binyon's best work belongs to the period between the
two wars, such as his odes, *The Sirens* and *The Idols*, and his
translation of Dante's *Divina Commedia* into *terza rima*. W. H.
Davies, never straying outside his direct nature poetry, continued to write lyrics which have a strong texture made out of
simple elements. At first sight he seems more liable to attack,
but no genuine estimate can ignore his authentic approach to
nature, unambitious perhaps, but as safe within its own limits
as the verse of Herrick. In a very different way Lascelles
Abercrombie achieved in *The Sale of Saint Thomas* (begun in
1911 and completed in 1930) a combination of the dramatic and
contemplative which has no relation to the easy formula under
which the 'Georgian School' of poetry has been condemned.

The poets who were most attacked were those who had
become the inheritors of the English romantic tradition. They
concurred with Wordsworth in the belief that poetry was 'the
spontaneous overflow of powerful emotions'. Instead of merely
ignoring the ugliness of industry, they were attempting at their

best to reassert an admiration for nature and the rural ways of life in an increasingly urbanized world. They gave genuine expression to the joy and beauty which they discovered in their personal experience. They had a certain unity of purpose, though naturally their allegiances were varied. Rupert Brooke, for instance, against whom much of the attack centred, was interested in John Donne's poetry and wrote a volume on Webster's tragedies. But it cannot be maintained that he was moved by these poets as were T. S. Eliot and a later generation. There is never a complete seriousness in his acceptance of Donne's influence on his poetry, while his exploration of Webster's world, though conducted with great ingenuity, leaves one with the conviction that he cannot have believed in its existence.

Rupert Brooke died on active service in the spring of 1915. He had not lived long enough for his poetry to reach maturity. So keenly had he reacted to life during the years of his youth that he had become a symbol of that whole generation, gracious, idealistic, romantic, confident, and accepting life with a genuine affection. In one of his last sonnets, so often repeated that its original impact has become almost meaningless, Rupert Brooke wrote:

> If I should die, think only this of me:
>   That there's some corner of a foreign field
> That is for ever England. There shall be
>   In that rich earth a richer dust concealed.

Ten years later at the close of his poem *The Hollow Men*, T. S. Eliot wrote:

> This is the way the world ends
> Not with a bang but a whimper.

In the contrast of those two passages can be seen a difference of mental outlook which gains emphasis and diverse illustration in the years between the wars. It is the end of confidence and self-assurance, and instead the enunciation of a mood which is near to despair. That change has emerged not from any individual fretfulness, or distress, but from a recognition of the general disruption of civilization. Whatever may be the verdict of future generations, for those who have lived through these decades the great writers are the genuinely creative artists who saw this crisis and attempted to express it in imaginative terms. Other writers however brilliant fall somehow short of the highest level if they ignore this spiritual crisis in man's history. This present study is an attempt to analyse some of the work of those who had this prophetic intuition.

CHAPTER II

THE LITERARY SCENE

IN thus discussing literature one must realize that attention is being concentrated on a few of the books published between the two wars, on those works solely which have shown an awareness of the contemporary situation. No attempt is made to describe as a whole the work published in these years. The selection, as far as authors are concerned, is, I realize, somewhat arbitrary, though inevitably so. I admit freely the delight and insight of much of the work I have excluded, but I would submit that it has not to any marked extent the prophetic or representative quality which I am seeking.

Throughout these years the production of books remained prolific, with fiction easily dominating. In 1919, 8,622 volumes were published : in 1922, 8,754. By 1939 this had increased to a grand total of 14,913, and this was a decrease of 1,178 on the output of 1938. It would be difficult to assess the influence of this vast book production as a whole. Many of the novels belonged to the category of work deliberately produced to meet the ·needs of an amply leisured audience of no outstanding intelligence which enjoyed seeing contemporary problems and emotions presented in fictional form. The lending libraries had constituted themselves into the means of distributing this material to large and widely scattered audiences, and the whole organization of the book and publishing trades was affected by the enormous book-borrowing public of fiction readers. This literature had been produced during all periods from the eighteenth century onwards, but with increased literacy the demand for it grew formidably in the years under review.

Some writers of erudition and genuine imaginative quality, such as Miss Dorothy Sayers, abandoned any attempt at stretching their qualities to the full in order to produce mystery and detective stories for the leisure reading of highly intelligent people. They brought to an idle and meretricious form all the talents that might have been used in a healthier period for great creative writing. Other writers, such as Sir Hugh Walpole, showed a capacity for narrative, ample and technically competent, which without any obvious adjustment on the author's part seemed to meet the values and needs of an easy-living and unexciting audience. It was as if the monotony of life, especially in the great urbanized areas, was producing a formidable number of readers who required to dull their intelligence with verbal entertainment, or who needed narratives whose sequences and values were easily assimilated. Further, fiction became a mirror for conduct and misconduct, and many who were restrained by convention to lives of routine and propriety found stimulus in reading of others who enjoyed richer emotional experiences, though in somewhat more disordered existences. Fiction became a confessional, a pulpit, and a stimulus, but fulfilled each function in a rather mild and ineffective way.

At the same time it is in fiction that are to be found within the period developments more marked and original than in any other form of literature, and though the work of the advanced experimenters is not widely read, it influences the more popular practitioners of the art. The study of psycho-analytical literature by novelists, while it has never been profound, gave them new liberties in vocabulary and new conceptions of form. Freud's work had been translated in part before the war of 1914-18, and while few novelists could have passed even an elementary examination on its content, they gained through him a sense that the conscious life was only a small part of man's existence, and that the mind instead of being ordered and logical was like a misbehaved and disordered menagerie. Further, they had accepted the conclusion that sex played a far larger place in man's life than had been previously conceived. They were encouraged to be bolder in the description of sexual experience and less affronted by sexual abnormalities. They were strengthened in their assault upon reticence by the possession of a technical vocabulary of whose precise clinical significance they were often unaware, but which served very much as a Latin text had done in the translation of the less seemly portions of the Classics.

Though Freud may be regarded as the centre of this psychological influence, it is clear that the study of psychology had long before entered into fiction in a number of other less direct ways. The assimilation of John Locke's speculations on the human mind in the seventeenth century had been in part responsible for the insight into man's conduct and his emotional life shown by the novelists of the eighteenth century. Though Richardson was not a philosopher, it can be urged that without Locke the subtle analysis of Richardson would have been impossible. In *Tristram Shandy* Sterne reached, though by a comic route, the conclusion that thought does not emerge from the mind in well-balanced sentences and ordered paragraphs and sometimes his genius gives to the planned disorder of his narrative a strangely modern feeling. The same experiments had been made in a more deliberate form by Edouard Dujardin in *Les lauriers sont coupés* of 1887. Dujardin was reproducing *le monologue intérieur*, the unspoken thoughts of the character as they tumbled one upon another in the free association of the unconscious mind. This is the device employed by Dorothy Richardson, Virginia Woolf and James Joyce. It is a method which was reinforced by the influence of the technique of the cinema, which with its frequent sequences could conquer time far more easily than the traditional drama.

At no period was the contrast more complete between the tastes and requirements of the general audience and the methods and achievements of the individual artists whose work had original and creative qualities. In 1922 T. S. Eliot's *The Waste Land* appeared in England after a previous publication in America, yet it met with little comment and some of that was hostile. The attention of the public that read poetry was elsewhere, for it was at this very time that collected editions appeared of the work of John Drinkwater, W. H. Davies and John Masefield. In the estimate of general taste during the period the year 1929 is particularly illuminating. In that year, for instance, *The Edinburgh Review*, which had existed since 1802, ' in order to accustom country gentlemen to the reading of books', ceased publication. Within a few months *The Listener* was on sale with its attempt to capture a new and more popular culture from the record of broadcasting talks. A public which was beginning to have the moral strength to recall and analyse the horrors of the war of 1914-18, welcomed the pseudo-realism of Remarque's *All Quiet on the Western Front*, while exploring at the same time the more genuine analysis of Richard Aldington's *Death of a Hero*, and Ernest Hemingway's documentary frankness in *A Farewell to Arms*. The public accepted Charles Morgan's elegant romanticism in the *Portrait in a Mirror* and crowded, with an enthusiasm unknown since Dickens had ceased to write, to read the encouraging mixture of humour and good-hearted adventure enjoyed by broad recognizable types in J. B. Priestley's *Good Companions*. In poetry the same public, or part of it, turned to buy Robert Bridges's philosophical poem *The Testament of Beauty*, until its sales became among the largest of any volume of verse in the inter-war years.

All the literature mentioned in the last paragraph is obviously of a high standard of accomplishment. Nor did the record of the year end there, for it included Edith Sitwell's *Gold Coast Customs* and Osbert Sitwell's *The Man Who Lost Himself*. The authors now mentioned, and others like them, were those that commanded the major part of the cultured and intelligent reading public in those years. The only limitation which can be suggested to these writers is that they did not realize that they lived in a crisis in human history. They went on competently, often brilliantly, with the methods which would have been adequate if life had been normal. This is what distinguishes them, in varying degrees, from the writers whom I have examined in greater detail. Some of those writers had less consistent talents, and less accomplishment, but they possessed some imaginative insight or intuition that told them that life was moving into a new era.

It is illuminating to remember that seven years before this year of 1929, Joyce's *Ulysses* had been published in Paris. It came in the very year that Galsworthy's *Forsyte Saga* was being published as a single volume. It fell upon the middle of the era when English realism, following Galsworthy and Arnold Bennett, was reproducing a fiction popular and accomplished, but missing in fresh creative power. The books that the English reading public favoured in 1921 were studies in a rather obvious realism such as F. Brett Young's *Black Diamond*, Hugh Walpole's *The Young Enchanted*, Sheila Kaye-Smith's *Joanna Godden*. It is true that there was more vital work from three women writers, in the satire of Rose Macaulay's *Dangerous Ages*, the bitter psychological study of May Sinclair's *Mr. Waddington of Wyck*, and the keen analysis of Rebecca West's *The Judge* (published in 1922). Yet given volumes such as these as generally representative of informed taste of the wider public in England it is not difficult to understand that there should have been so little appreciation of the audacious, and at times tormented vision of *Ulysses*.

Whatever may be one's ultimate judgement upon it as a work of art, few will any longer deny that James Joyce's *Ulysses* is one of the most outstanding and original prose works of the period. The conditions of its publication show how far removed it was from the accomplished literature which even the more intelligent contributors to the circulating libraries were reading. It was first published serially in *The Little Review*, in New York. The fifth issue was seized and condemned for obscenity. The complete work was published in Paris in 1922. The Egoist Press, London, issued two editions, and while copies of the first were burned by the New York Post Office authorities, the destruction of the second fell to the lot of the Custom authorities in Folkestone. Pirated editions appeared freely in America, and led in 1927 to a plea by a large number of writers for the free issue of the book. Finally in 1933 the ban was removed. The speech in which the American judge issued his sentence may well become historic. 'In *Ulysses*,' he said, 'in spite of its unusual frankness I do not detect anywhere the leer of the sensualist. I hold that it is not pornographic . . . The words which are construed as dirty are old Saxon words known to almost all men, I venture, to many women, and are such words as would be naturally and habitually used, I believe, by the types of folk whose life, physical and mental, Joyce is seeking to describe.' At long last, in 1936, *Ulysses* was published for the first time in a regular way in England, though in a very expensive edition. Such was the history of a work of original imagination, around which a considerable critical literature had appeared. In years during which it struggled first for existence and then for recognition the average annual production of books was over ten thousand volumes.

This contrast of the vast production of books and the limited circulation of works of original imagination makes it difficult to assess the place of literature in modern society. Indeed it can be urged that in the years under review all reading matter has had a declining place in the interests of the population of this country as a whole. The development of radio as a public service belongs to these years, and as a consequence the spoken word in talks, plays and discussions has occupied a far larger place in popular attention than ever before. In this same period between the two wars the film added a sound track to its visual appeal and became by far the most extensive medium for the transmission of drama. Indeed only through these two media can literature be said to have entered into the lives of the community as a whole. It may well be that literary criticism as an independent entity should cease, and should be replaced by a cultural criticism which would include literature, drama, the film and the radio as parts of one single activity. In both radio and the film, work of great artistic brilliance was achieved, but at the same time those who controlled these instruments were very conscious of the vast audience to which they appealed, and were anxious, indeed far too anxious, to make concessions to the alleged lowness of the average intelligence.

Nor did this awareness of the mass audience confine itself to the masters of the radio and the film. The proprietors of the press, unceasingly in pursuit of larger circulations and dogged by the claims of advertisers, made ever-increasing concessions to what they believed to be the strongest desires of the greatest number. The space allotted in the daily press to the criticism of books, and art, and music steadily declined until in some journals it became almost non-existent. When *A Shropshire Lad* was first published in 1896 Richard le Gallienne gave it a whole column review on the front page of *The Star*. Such conduct by any newspaper in 1922 when A. E. Housman's *Last Poems* were published would be inconceivable. In *The Star*, at the end of the eighties, G. B. Shaw attended to *Music* and William Archer to *Drama*, apart from the column given to literature. All this was contrived despite the fact that the paper was only a four-page news-sheet and committed to a policy of making the widest popular appeal, and issued at a halfpenny.

The conditions of modern life, particularly of urban life, were making the act of reading more difficult than, say in the nineteenth century, when a long work such as Macaulay's *History* could command a large audience. The competing claims on leisure had increased, so that life was more mobile and the attractions of a variety of entertainments became more persistent. The middle-class family which once had a good library now had a small car. The book had to enter into a competitive market in order to make its claims heard. Ruskin had already called the nineteenth century a bill-poster age, but this was far more true of the twentieth. Some writers, particularly the historians, and biographers such as Lytton Strachey and Philip Guedalla, tried to make their style an agent of salesmanship for the goods they had to offer.

As has already been suggested, seldom was there a period when such a marked difference separates the writers of more original imagination from those whose work was more the product of talent guided by imitation. Beneath them both were the purveyors of 'trades goods' for the masses. This last group can, of course, be easily distinguished, but in this period it is difficult to attempt a comparative assessment of the achievement of talent from the genuinely original. Often the more conventional work is more interesting, more reassuring, and one is perplexed why it does not signify more than it does. Only gradually does one become aware of the fact that it no longer answers the new, strange, harsh shape in which the world and civilization show themselves. It is the product of minds who still live in the pattern of a past which is no longer there.

The genuinely original work arising from a knowledge that whatever happens the old values will not return, is often dissatisfying, but the weaknesses arise from the supreme task of seeking a new medium for a new range of experience. The problem is complicated, as it is indeed in all the arts, by the fact that it is easier for the spurious practitioners to imitate works of original genius, which are still struggling to discover their own true form, than to produce works of talent in the traditional manner. Especially in a period such as this, when the emphasis has lain on experiment, and when the works resulting have all been 'difficult', and when the elements comprising the ' difficult ' have not been easily soluble by reason, the dishonest and the incompetent can more easily gain acceptance for their wares. There has undoubtedly been much incompetence and wilful eccentricity and some have mistaken unnecessary obscurity for the strange new pattern which original genius has created. Even among those who have possessed some original creative force there has been a danger of self-sufficiency, fed by the plaudits of a small minority who have studied and unravelled their work with uncritical enthusiasm.

For whatever the differences which separate the mature work of T. S. Eliot, James Joyce and Virginia Woolf, it can at least be conceded that on its first appearance all their work was ' difficult '. Arnold Bennett was only reflecting the views of many ordinary readers when he said that James Joyce's *Ulysses* was the work which first made novel-reading a form of penal servitude, while E. M. Forster commented ironically on the same view by saying that no one understood *Ulysses*, not even the police who prohibited its circulation. *Ulysses* was followed by the far more difficult *Finnegans Wake*, a volume which made the earlier work seem a mere primer in unintelligibility. This element of difficulty was inevitable, but it showed that there was no easy communication between the artist and the society in which he lived. There was in fact no conception of a homogeneous community. The absence of that understanding is an indication of the uneasy and fragmentary condition of the modern mind. I would here reaffirm a conviction that however inevitable the complexity and difficulty of modern art may be there can be no condition of health until large numbers of people find themselves able to appreciate art without difficulty and without any conscious concession or adjustment on the part of the artist.

It can, of course, be suggested that the enjoyment of art is an exercise only for the few, but this is a conclusion from which Michelangelo, Shakespeare, and indeed most of the greatest artists of the past would have dissented. There is a danger throughout the period that a small audience revenges itself on the inadequacy of life by enjoying a literature which it realizes is too complex for ordinary readers to understand. Similarly there are artists who are content with the manipulation of a difficult medium, without employing it for any great purpose. They substitute dexterity in technique for creation. Both the poets and the novelists suffer from this confusion. It arises in part from the old unrest which the artist has ever felt in the middle of a commercial society, and more profoundly in a sense that the spirit of man has lost its way in the wilderness of modern living.

In the thirties there was an attempt, particularly among the younger poets, to broaden their approach. John Garrett and W. H. Auden in their preface to *The Poet's Tongue* describe poetry as ' memorable speech ' and add that ' the test of a poet is the frequency and diversity of the occasions on which we remember his poetry '. This anthology was published in 1935, and though the views expressed are not original they are interesting, particularly as far as Auden is concerned. For they stand as an expression by one who was then a leader of the younger generation of the need for a more intelligible and sociable art. ' Artistic creations ', the editors said, ' may be produced by individuals, and because their work is only appreciated by a few it does not necessarily follow that it is not good; but a universal art can only be the product of a community united in sympathy, sense of worth, and aspiration, and it is improbable that the artist can do his best except in such a society.'

There was, of course, nothing new in this conception. For Matthew Arnold had spoken in a very similar way in the opening essay of *Essays in Criticism: First Series*: ' In the Greece of Pindar and Sophocles, in the England of Shakespeare, the poet lived in a current of ideas in the highest degree animating and nourishing to the creative power : society was, in the fullest measure, permeated by fresh thought, intelligent and alive.' The same view can indeed be found again in Trotsky's *Literature and Revolution*: 'Art is not a disembodied element feeding on itself, but a function of social man indissolubly tied to his life and environment.' Particularly during the Spanish Civil War the poets felt an urgent desire to communicate with their audiences, and this led to a directness and clarification of their work. It may further be noted that when the first All-Union Congress of Soviet Writers met in 1934 there was an attack on all stylistic complications of form. Joyce's *Ulysses* was quoted as an extreme example. It was suggested that these devices were an indication not of any genuine qualities but of bourgeois decadence.

It must be admitted that many original and strong minds in the inter-war period gave way to a feeling that was negative and akin to despair. They saw no cause to which their energy could be attached and consequently developed a bitter and frustrated spirit. They felt that charity and expediency in social experiment could not remedy the suffering aroused from a misadjusted economic system, and that in the international field the policy of the Government was so enervating that protest was futile. As a result men of considerable ability were for the last ten or twenty years using their talents to no constructive purpose. If they had shared a faith they would have been organized, but without a faith they lived in bitter isolation. When they were writers the marks of these unhappy conclusions are to be seen clearly in their work. Their own frustration found its only expression in their satire and mockery of the modern world. England seemed to them to have no common aim and men were in danger of viewing each other with distrust and disparagement.

An example of the portrayal of this mood can be seen in George Orwell's *Coming Up for Air*, which tells of an ex-officer of the war of 1914-18, who becomes an insurance agent, and lives meanly in a minute suburban house, with behind it

C

'ten yards by five of grass, with a privet hedge round it and a bare patch in the middle, that we call the back garden. There's the same back garden, same privets and same grass, behind every house in Ellesmere Road.' The same type of figure had been portrayed by Dickens and by H. G. Wells in *Kipps*, but while Dickens had humour, compassion and faith and Wells humour and an expectation from the future, Orwell had mockery only, a disdainful, helpless mockery that arose ultimately from despair. With Dickens and Wells one felt that life was cruel but that men could still unite in the struggle for its improvement, Orwell implied that all that was best in the English tradition had merged into a meaningless succession of Ellesmere Roads, which in a mood of bitter and unrelieved cynicism he now contemplated without any vestige of hope remaining.

I am not condemning George Orwell's novel which is a very remarkable book, and in the post-war England he has spoken with a new and more positive voice. I quote his work as an expression, by a highly intelligent mind, of the negative and frustrated ways of the pre-war years. Throughout the novel one must remember, also, that it is Mr. Orwell's ex-officer of the 1914-18 war who is speaking and not Orwell himself. Here is the voice of his hero as he approaches London in a car, and contemplates the city; 'and presently I struck into outer London and followed the Uxbridge Road as far as Southall. Miles and miles of ugly houses, with people living dull, decent lives inside them. And beyond it London, stretching on and on, streets, squares, back-alleys, tenements, blocks of flats, pubs, fried-fish shops, picture houses, on and on for twenty miles, and all the eight million people with their little private lives which they don't want to have altered. . . . And the chaos of it. The privateness of all those lives!' Later he comments on what will happen to it when war comes again : 'I only know that if there's anything you care a curse about better say good-bye to it now, because everything you've ever known is going down, down, into the muck with the machine-guns rattling all the time.' The sentiment of this passage was reiterated by a number of intelligent minds who faced the future with despair : 'Everything you've ever known is going down.' If unity is to be discovered in the varied work within the period it will be found in an increasing recognition of the degree to which civilization has been disrupted. Few of the genuinely creative minds offer any complete or satisfying solution of the dilemma. They are able to diagnose the disease of their age without the strength to heal it.

At the same time there can be seen a growing strength and confidence among writers whose standpoint is definitely Christian. Of major importance here has been the degree of accomplishment of certain Roman Catholic writers. Gerard Manley Hopkins died as early as 1889, but the public did not become aware of his poetry until Robert Bridges issued an edition of the *Poems* in 1918. Even then attention fastened only slowly on his work and sales were very poor, so that a second edition, under Charles Williams's editorship, was not called for until 1930. Hopkins, by his prosodic theories and his inventions in form and in the use of vocabulary, commanded sympathy among many younger men who were unmoved by his Christian allegiances. Yet others discovered in his work for the first time the nature of religious experience, and came to respect the faith more because they now learned here how deeply it had affected one whom they admired on other grounds.

G. K. Chesterton, who died in 1936, and Hilaire Belloc belong to an earlier tradition of Roman Catholic writing. They were both active in the inter-war period, but it is not unjust to say that their major effectiveness belonged to an earlier day. For Chesterton it can be found in 1908 when he wrote *Orthodoxy*, or 1917 when he published his highly individual *Short History of England*. With Belloc the most active period probably extends from 1902 when *The Path to Rome* appeared to *The Servile State* in 1912. There was a revival of Chesterton's influence with the appearance after his death of an excellent biographical study and the publication of some revealing autobiographical material.

To a younger generation the positive effect of Christianity on literature gained its strongest adherent in T. S. Eliot whose pageant play, *The Rock*, appeared in 1934. Eliot probably lost some of his earlier followers by this firm allegiance to the Anglican Church, though he discovered a new audience, especially with *Murder in the Cathedral*, 1935. There have also been other writers who, beginning with secular themes, have brought distinguished ability to the union of their creative talents and Christian theological studies. In the later years of the war, and in the period immediately following, an outstanding example has been C. S. Lewis. All the exceptional insight which he possessed as a critic has been united to an imaginative power in popularizing Christian apologetics with all the armoury of a well-equipped layman. Further, there are ample indications among younger writers that this Christian approach will continue.

While this Christian movement in imaginative literature exists, and may indeed be increasing, many writers have never been able to share in it. They perceive the lack of integration in their own lives, and they perceive Western civilization threatened by its own spiritual weakness. The new barbarism makes its own confident inroads, and Western civilization seems not to possess the mind or the weapons to offer adequate resistance. They seem to see the writers of Christian conviction as capable of satisfying only a group of adherents, while being helpless to change the shape of society as a whole. With the majority of the more original minds the choice of varied and difficult media is an expression of their awareness that they are moving into a new and difficult era.

CHAPTER III

E. M. FORSTER

IN this and the following chapters I have selected for more detailed treatment five novelists. I admit freely that others have achieved great success in the novel in the period and on this I have already commented. At the same time I would submit, following the argument I have already developed, that these are the five writers who are most alive to the most profound problem of their time, and whose work either directly through comment and discussion as with Huxley or Lawrence, or indirectly as in Joyce or Virginia Woolf is an image of the age.

It may at first sight seem improper to include E. M. Forster for he was writing as early as 1905 and, apart from short stories, only one of his works, *A Passage to India*, falls within the period. Yet his influence was throughout considerable and admiration for his work has increased with the years. Further, he is the supreme example of the very aristocracy of liberal intellectualism, undeluded by the tenets it had maintained earlier in the century and adjusting its sense of reality to the changing shape of the world.

In the fiction of the period E. M. Forster, who was born in 1879, holds an altogether exceptional place. He neither assaults the reader with a new creed as does Lawrence, nor stalks forth clad aggressively in technical novelties. His methods, it is true, are new, but they are immediately intelligible. He has come to hold a position as high as any one in these decades and this despite the fact that his production has been so small. Success has certainly not tempted him to increase it. The interest taken in his work in the United States has been considerable and is shown by the able study of a young American critic, Lionel Trilling, whose volume *E. M. Forster* (1945) shows an unusual knowledge of the English background. Forster's earliest novel *Where Angels Fear to Tread* appeared in 1905. There followed *The Longest Journey* in 1907, and *A Room with a View*, with which his reputation was first established, was published in the following year. Then in 1910 came *Howard's End*, a novel of great power and beauty, which attracted wide attention.

As a result of his work in Alexandria during the war of 1914-18 he published a guide and history of the city, but it was only in 1924, after an interval of fourteen years, that he completed another work of fiction, *A Passage to India*, which immediately took its place as one of the most brilliant novels of the period. Since then he has not published any further work in fiction, apart from some short stories in *The Eternal Moment* (1928). He had already published a volume of short stories entitled *The Celestial Omnibus* as early as 1911. Even *The Eternal Moment*, though it was published in 1928, contains solely work that was published before 1914 and has the prefatory note that it contains 'all that the writer is likely to attempt in a particular line'.

Forster belonged to the tradition of cultured liberalism at its best. In his early years when conditions domestically, and in Europe, seemed tolerably secure he did not intrude into politics, but he loved the civilization which the liberal tradition had created, and the opportunities for leisure and personal relations which it gave. Even in those early years he realized, as can now be seen in *Howard's End*, that there were whole classes excluded from the advantages of the privileged minority. Already in that early period his reactions explore the nature of the human personality, and the conception of the civilized life, with moods that vary from social comedy to the graver reflections on the idea of Death, and with never an absence of the knowledge that life is a strange and mystical experience into which intrude moments that are cruel, disconcerting and befouled.

In the later years, when Fascism had raised its ugly head, and when the methods and conclusions of Communism were apparent, he saw that the way of life which he had favoured might be an oasis rather than an enduring possibility. Yet his acute awareness and frank freshness in facing the future protected him from any self-pity, weakness or nostalgia. So in 1934 he wrote, that there is ' the present order, which I prefer, because I have been brought up in it. I like Parliament and democracy. I should like England and Europe to muddle on as they are, without the international explosion that would end them. . . . In the second place, there is Communism, an alternative which will destroy all I care for and could only be reached through violence, yet it might mean a new order where younger people could be happy and the head and the heart have a chance to grow. There, and on no other horizon, the boys and girls might return to the cliff and dance. If my own world smashes, Communism is what I would like in its place, but I shall not bless it until I die. And, thirdly, there is Fascism, leading only into the blackness which it has chosen as its symbol, into smartness and yapping out of orders, and self-righteous brutality, into social as well as international war.'

His education had been that of the more favoured elements in the middle classes. He had been to school at Tonbridge, which if it is to be identified with the Sawston of the novels, yielded him experiences which he hated. On the other hand, at King's College, Cambridge, he came into something which was more than an institution. It constituted for him a way of life, the spirit that is genuine and lively and cultured and playful. In all the novels there is an opposition between evil, which is cruel, philistine and unperceiving, and the good, which is lively, entertaining and sensitive. For him, Cambridge, and particularly King's College, was the supreme symbol of the civilized approach : ' Body and spirit, reason and emotion, work and play, architecture and scenery, laughter and seriousness, life and art—these pairs which are elsewhere contrasts were there fused into one. People and books reinforced one another, intelligence joined hands with affection, speculation became a passion, and discussion was made profound by love.'

Forster had much that went beyond this cultured liberal tradition. He had travelled in India with Lowes Dickinson, whose biography he published in 1934, and had assimilated from the East a conception of personality that eliminated all the Faustian elements which the West so admired. The aim of the civilized life would be to enhance the quality of personal relations. That would not be achieved by pomp and power and aggressiveness in the personality, but by gentle and quiescent qualities. As the years pass and Europe degenerates towards barbarism, this gentleness seems less effective than once it did, but Forster himself is aware of this and is not deluded by what is happening in this new and crueller world.

While all his work has this extraordinary lightness of touch and this sensitive spirit, it is not weak and never sentimental. Death comes suddenly and unexpectedly to his characters, and part of Forster's philosophy is that the contemplation of the idea of death is necessary to the good life. ' Death destroys a man : the idea of Death saves him ! Behind the coffins and the skeletons, that stay the vulgar mind, lies something so immense that all that is great in us responds to it. Men of the world may recoil from the charnel-house that they will one day enter, but Love knows better. Death is his foe, but his peer, and in their age-long struggle the thews of Love have been strengthened, and his vision cleared until there is no one who can stand against him.' Nor do the capacities of man for anger and passion and cruelty escape him. They are shown, most melodramatically, in the earliest novel, *Where Angels*

Fear to Tread, where the young Italian, Gino, hearing of his child's death, displays an obscene passion which includes an attempt at murder. Though there are few scenes in the later novels which indulge so openly in horror, the elements of violence and evil are never obscured.

With all this brilliance of incident and dialogue Forster remains throughout a moralist. This may be less obvious since his morality is individual and has a philosophy and a mystical background. He distinguishes throughout between the civilized and the barbarous, between those who have a room with a view and those who have not. The theme is to be found everywhere in his work. He expresses it with great delicacy and imagination. Thus in *Howard's End* we are shown Helen listening to Beethoven's Fifth Symphony : ' " Look out for the part where you think you have done with the goblins and they come back," breathed Helen, as the music started with a goblin walking quietly over the universe, from end to end. Others followed him. They were not aggressive creatures; it was that that made them so terrible to Helen. They merely observed in passing that there was no such thing as splendour or heroism in the world. . . . Beethoven chose to make it all right in the end. He built the ramparts up. He blew with his mouth for the second time, and again the goblins were scattered. He brought back the gusts of splendour, the heroism, the youth, the magnificence of life and of death, and, amid roarings of a superhuman joy he led his Fifth Symphony to its conclusion. But the goblins were there. They could return. He said so bravely, and that is why one can trust Beethoven when he says other things.' In such descriptions he suggests the eternal conflict in life between those who seek individual lives and true individual relations and the quest of beauty, and those who want power, and property, and high office.

Sometimes with a startling suddenness he will intrude a description of this perpetual and hostile duality in life. After some passage of incident and dialogue it will come in with a quality that is poetical and mystical. So at the conclusion of one of the episodes in *Howard's End* he writes : 'England was alive, throbbing through all her estuaries, crying for joy through the mouths of all her gulls, and the north wind, with contrary motion, blew stronger against her rising seas. What did it mean? For what end are her fair complexities, her changes of soil, her sinuous coast? Does she belong to those who have moulded her and made her feared by other lands, or to those who have added nothing to her power, but have somehow seen her, seen the whole island at once, lying as a jewel in a silver sea, sailing as a ship of souls, with all the brave world's fleet accompanying her towards eternity? '

All this, of course, would not make him a novelist. For that, fortunately, he had other resources. Above all he possessed a great power of story-telling which was denied to so many of his contemporaries. In 1927 he delivered the Clark Lectures at Cambridge on *Aspects of the Novel* and there he says : 'Yes—oh dear yes—the novel tells a story.' Of the nature of the story he adds : ' It can have one merit : that of making the audience want to know what happens next. And conversely it can only have one fault : that of making the audience not want to know what happens next.' So, as frequently in the novels, these statements follow the plan of saying something profoundly important in a light, almost colloquial manner. It may, at first reading, disguise the fact that *Aspects of the Novel* is one of the most important works of criticism on the art of fiction that has appeared in the period.

Though in his criticism he seems to deplore the necessity of plot, Forster can tell his story supremely well. Further, he can create character, with many shades and complexities, and with sensitive, lightly placed touches. This character-drawing is present from the first, though it matures in *Howard's End* and *A Passage to India*. Indeed it can be conceded that the portrait of Dr. Aziz, the young Mohammedan in *A Passage to India*, is the most revealing picture of an Indian ever drawn by an English writer, and one of the most subtle and convincing portraits in the whole period.

He had further a gift very rarely possessed, of rhythmic prose which in the novels seems as natural as conversation. This effect can only be achieved by an ear that can isolate from ordinary speech the movements that have ease and grace. It is a prose from which all obscurity and all weight have been removed. It falls easily upon the ear, and whenever it turns to conversation has an idiom at hand to capture each speaker. It can be varied from rich and poetical movements to phrases plucked fresh from common speech. This contrast is often used with great effect, as is the sudden change from a quiet domestic scene to violence or death. In *Howard's End* he can vary from the colloquial of ' Evie heard of her father's engagement when she was in for a tennis tournament, and her play went simply to pot ', to the bold and poetical quality of such a sentence as ' Let squalor be turned into Tragedy, whose eyes are the stars, and whose hands hold the sunset and the dawn '.

Ultimately Forster was possessed of an ironic spirit which made him the inheritor in this age of the tradition of comedy which he exercised with all Meredith's skill, though with a far lighter touch. Such comedy has shades which are whimsical and moments that are fantastic, while often the governing mood is gentleness, as of one whose gesture is deliberately unemphatic. But ever the reader is reminded that the gentleness arises from the certainty that the desired effect will be achieved. The surgeon is gentle as he uses the knife at a delicate moment in his operation, and at such a moment he knows, as does Forster, that all life and death is in his hand.

Much of his power as a story-teller was already present in *Where Angels Fear to Tread*, which he published in 1905 at the age of twenty-six. He is here more strident and melodramatic than later, but he has mastered the distinctive and sudden intrusion of ferocity and death with which he can catch the reader disturbingly unawares, and he has already the disconcerting mixture of comedy with violence and tragedy. His theme, which anticipates his later work, is the contrast of two cultures, of the English provincials and Italy, and yet not that simply, for there is also the contrast of two Italies, the one imagined by idealistic admirers and the other of the young Italian Gino, lazy, passionate, with a deep Latin desire for parenthood. So, as often in Forster, the simple contrast which should reduce the novel to a formula becomes involved in other contrasts until the whole work, while retaining its moral, becomes a vivid image of life itself.

The contrast appears again in *The Longest Journey* (1907), which is a novel of friendship, and of a bitterly unhappy marriage, of falsehoods and shams, and of the good life. The skill in character presentation is already there and the sense of rhythm in prose. Elements that are autobiographical must have contributed to the pictures of Sawston and of Cambridge. The portrait of the woman who is responsible for the unhappy marriage has a bitterness which is rare in the later books. It is as if the author were shaken by the crudity of the character he had created, while later he remains disconcertingly passive whatever the characters may do. The volume is heavier and more solemn than is common in the later works where comedy and the tragic come so impressively together.

A Room with a View (1908) is the volume with which Forster reaches full maturity. Without any violent departure from the traditional form of the novel he has discovered his own values and his own methods of portraying character and incident. His touch is never as light as here, and much of the novel has all the qualities of a social comedy. Yet the more serious meaning, or rather a series of meanings, is never obscure. As Miss Rose Macaulay has suggested, the central motive has the simplicity of a morality play. Of the guests in an Italian boarding-house, there are those who can distinguish the genuine from the false, and there are those who have no such insight. There are those who understand themselves and those who are caught in self-deception. The theme is made very clear by Forster's own comments. As he says of one of his characters: 'It did not do to think, nor, for the matter of that, to feel. She gave up trying to understand herself, and joined the vast armies of the benighted, who follow neither the heart nor the brain, and march to their destiny by catch-words. The armies are full of pleasant and pious folk. But they have yielded to the only enemy that matters—the enemy within.' It was as if he were restating the theme of *Where Angels Fear to Tread*, with the melodrama omitted.

Howard's End followed in 1910, and there Forster reached his highest achievement as a writer of fiction. It may be that the novelty of the setting will give *A Passage to India* a wider appeal, but the earlier novel has an equal strength of vision and ingenuity, and great variety in incident and character. The simplest definition of the theme is that it shows the contrast of those who live in a civilized world and those who do not; those who are on the side of the goblins and those who are not. Yet no longer, as in *A Room with a View*, can the novel be said to have the simplicity of a morality play. The variety of character and the complexity of motive dissolve the moral into the action. So he has made the whole novel a symbol of his plea that civilization depends on a world of discerning people.

Forster's sympathy with those who see life as 'personal relations' never leads him to handle his theme crudely. In an illuminating passage he makes Margaret Schegel, one of his most sensitive characters, say to her sister: 'I've often thought about it, Helen. It's one of the most interesting things in the world. The truth is that there is a great outer life that you and I have never touched—a life in which telegrams and anger count. Personal relations, that we think supreme, are not supreme there. There, love means marriage settlements, death, death duties. So far I'm clear. But here is my difficulty. This outer life, though obviously horrid, often seems the real one—there's grit in it. It does breed character. Do personal relations lead to sloppiness in the end? '

On the other hand the whole spirit of the book goes out most poetically to support those who seek the private life in all its honesty and radiance for ' it is the private life that holds out the mirror to infinity : personal intercourse and that alone, that ever hints at personality beyond our daily vision '. So varied is the suggestion of this novel that it cannot be caught into any brief description. *Howard's End* is the name of a house, but more than that, it is the name of a way of life that knows tradition, and loves the past and instinctively avoids all the false pretensions. The whole novel is a mirror of the period before 1914-18. Even the most evil in this novel could not have conceived of Fascism. The best of the people in the middle classes on which he concentrates are aware of their privileges and are seeking, sometimes clumsily, sometimes tragically, how they can help those who lie on the fringes of their world. Yet their assistance, and indeed their consciousness of society, extend only to the lowest elements in the middle class. Of the vast proletarian world they have no knowledge, but their author is aware of their ignorance and does not wholly share it.

As has already been suggested, *A Passage to India* has nothing technically to give it precedence over *Howard's End*, and some have preferred the earlier book. At the same time in this novel Forster has appealed to a very much larger audience than previously, and has achieved a genuine picture of Indians and of the English in India in a way which no other writer has found possible. His descriptive powers have greater opportunities in India, in the Malabar caves and in other scenes with a strange fresh background. He has escaped into a background which, unlike that of the earlier novels, most of his readers do not share. Further, India yielded him a supreme example of the importance of personal relations. For on this Eastern setting they have an almost mystical quality, and in a poignant and tragic contrast Forster is able to show the way in which men meet and lacerate each other because they fail to understand.

The Indian scene brought out with greater clarity his irony and kindliness, and his power of slipping suddenly within a sentence from the colloquial to the sublime. The subtle way in which thought and comment are mingled into the language and lives of his characters is present everywhere. So of Mrs. Moore he writes that she felt ' that she had made a mistake in mentioning God, but she found Him increasingly difficult to avoid as she grew older, and He had been constantly in her thoughts since she entered India, though oddly enough He satisfied her less '. The atmosphere is certainly richer and more varied here than elsewhere, as Forster gives that world of strange odours and colours, of the splendour and unexpected-ness, of the beautiful and the terrifying, which is India. Some-times this enters into the very texture of the narrative itself and is conveyed by the lightest touches, or by the conversation, but there are other passages where he speaks with a more conscious, even rhetorical, movement. So he writes of the Indian heat : ' All over the city and over much of India the same retreat on the part of humanity was beginning, into cellars, up hills, under trees. April, herald of horrors, is at hand. The sun was returning to his kingdom with power but without beauty— that was the sinister feature. If only there had been beauty ! His cruelty would have been tolerable then. Through excess of light, he failed to triumph, he also; in his yellow-white over-flow not only matter, but brightness itself lay drowned.'

It is this strange atmosphere, fascinating and yet sinister, which gives to the re-expression of the philosophy an enhanced sense of the poignant. The ' goblins ' are here too, and those who seek enlightenment, and those who are enamoured of the dark ways, but it has all been made more complex for those who seek the good life by the barriers of civilization, of race, and creed, of caste, and of all the complex relations of the

British and the Indian. Mrs. Moore sees it all after her weary-ing visit to the Malabar caves with the disconsolate ' ou-boum ' of their echo : ' The crush and the smells she could forget, but the echo began in some indescribable way to undermine her hold on life. Coming at a moment when she chanced to be fatigued it had managed to murmur, " Pathos, piety, courage—they exist but are identical, and so is filth. Everything exists, nothing has value." If one had spoken vileness in that place, or quoted lofty poetry, the comment would have been the same.'

Apart from the novel and short stories, and *Aspects of the Novel*, Forster's quality comes through in his collection of essays, *Abinger Harvest* (1936), and in his guide-book and history of Alexandria. This is a strangely beautiful narrative, one in which the quality of his style, in its lightness and evocative power, is admirably shown. He reconstructs the past with economy and dramatic skill and the ironical mood still finds opportunity in legend and history and current comment.

Though so little of his work has appeared in the years between the two wars he has established himself securely as one of the outstanding writers of his age. In a period when neologisms in form were boisterous his supreme craftsmanship permitted him to work more quietly, as if his manners were too good for the elaborate antics of some of his contemporaries. He never relaxed from his vision of the man of good taste, able to exercise his senses and his talents, and maintain his faith that civilization is the sum of such men and women existing in an unorganized unity. His conception of this last and funda-mental element in his philosophy and faith has almost a mystical quality.

Everywhere in his work, in the novels and essays alike, he returns to emphasize this importance of the individual life. It appears in a memorable passage in one of his essays, where he describes reading Huysman's *A Rebours* during the war of 1914-18 : ' Oh, the relief of a world which lived for its sensations and ignored the will—the world of des Esseintes! Was it decadent? Yes, and thank God. Yes; here was a human being who had time to feel and experiment with his feelings, to taste and arrange books and fabricate flowers, and be selfish and himself. The waves of edifying bilge rolled off one, the newspapers ebbed; Professor Cramb, that profound philosopher, and Raemaekers, that inspired artist, floated out into an oblivion which, thank God, has since become permanent, and something resembling reality took their place. Perhaps it was not real, but it was helpful, and in 1917 that was enough to make me repeat after the muezzin in my minaret, " Thank God! " ' This faith in the individual, affirmed so strongly and yet without sentimentality, has an obvious importance in this period. Nor can one easily conceive that the attractiveness of his view of life will diminish, even when it is less attainable. This, combined with his supreme effectiveness, gives him the more secure promise of a permanent and high place among the writers of English fiction.

D

CHAPTER IV

JAMES JOYCE

OF all writers in the period a claim can be made that James Joyce may be considered one of those most concerned with what Eliot described as ' that small part of " literature " which is really creative '. Around him the fiercest literary controversies of these decades have raged, though few now who are interested in literature would deny his complete integrity as an artist, and his stature as a genius, even though of a strange and bewildering order. His early volume of short stories, *The Dubliners*, is direct in method, simple in vocabulary, and though powerfully evocative in incident and mood, shows none of the complex qualities which surround his later work. *A Portrait of the Artist as a Young Man* (1916) was the novel through which for a long time he was best known in England. It is a very moving account, in part obviously autobiographical, of Stephen Dedalus, brought up in a Jesuit school, and breaking with Catholicism because he feels within him the desires of an artist for beauty. Naturalistic in method, it is conveyed movingly, and confronts the reader with no technical difficulties, though it is written in a fresh and individual way. Readers of *A Portrait* could not be prepared for the technical developments which were to follow, though on looking back one can discover present already the mental attitude which governed Joyce in later years.

The circumstances that attended the publication of *Ulysses* (1922) have already been described. How far the campaign of vilification was extended is illustrated by J. Isaacs in his appendix to Louis Golding's study of *James Joyce* : ' The strangest episode in Joyce's difficult progress towards recognition was revealed in the Centenary Exhibition of the *Revue des Deux Mondes* when a letter was shown dated June 7th, 1924, and signed E. Gosse : " My dear Monsieur Gillet, I should very much regret your paying Mr. J. Joyce the compliment of an article in the *Revue des Deux Mondes*. You could only expose the worthlessness and impudence of his writings, and surely it would be a mistake to give him the prominence. I have difficulty in describing to you in writing the character of Mr. Joyce's notoriety. It is partly political; it is partly a perfectly cynical appeal to sheer indecency. He is of course not entirely without talent, but he is a literary . . ." The remainder of the letter was not visible.'

Ulysses is based on what happened in the mind and life of Leopold Bloom in a period of twenty-four hours in Dublin on June 16th 1904. Numerous characters are introduced, including Stephen Dedalus, while the volume concludes with the soliloquy of Mrs. Marion Bloom, one of the most notorious but moving episodes in the whole work. The *Odyssey* is used as a basis for the design, and episodes in the epic have their counterpart in the modern chronicle. It is difficult to assess the precise value of this machinery of reference to the classical epic. Often it appears, as so much else in Joyce's work, as an effort of wit, existing alongside, and occasionally even supplanting the creative intention. At the same time the formal pattern of the epic must have given some sustaining structure on which to base his explorations into the wildernesses of the human mind. Beyond all this one may be allowed to suspect a satirical, or even philosophical intention. Joyce is contrasting the adventure, and mystery, and the romance of the classical epic, with the sordid and trivial existence of his own characters. Life instead of being full of adventure has become an inward life of unilluminated frustration, and of disconsolate and furtive emotional relief. Rather it can be said that Joyce partly by incident, but more by vocabulary and associative reference, has given his work a unity similar to that of a musical composition. The Homeric parallel may in this have assisted him, though I doubt if it is as essential to his purpose as is often suggested. It is, like some of the effects of language in *Hamlet*, an affair of wit carried on, along with main design, and interesting in itself, but largely for a separate life and vitality of its own.

Ulysses is the culmination of the influence of psychology on the novel. Such influence was present, though not in so elaborate a way, in Dorothy Richardson, whose first chronicle of Miriam's mind was published as *Pointed Roofs* in 1915. In some form this psychological knowledge has affected most modern literature, and often in a deliberate and conscious way, as in the work of Virginia Woolf. With Joyce this influence is at once more elaborate and profound. He had been at Zurich during the years of the first world war, and there he had written *Ulysses* in the very headquarters of Jung's psycho-analytic movement. To this can be added philosophical influences from Bergson and Whitehead, so that as one of the most acute of his critics, H. Levin, writes in *James Joyce, A Critical Introduction* : 'The very form of Joyce's book is an elusive and eclectic *Summa* of its age : the *montage* of the cinema, impressionism in painting, *leit-motif* in music, the free association of psycho-analysis, and vitalism in philosophy. Take of these elements all that is fusible, and perhaps more, and you have the style of *Ulysses*.' As far as there was a direct precedent it was to be found in the work of Edouard Dujardin, and Joyce has acknowledged his debt to Dujardin's *Les lauriers sont coupés*.

Joyce, like Eliot, is trying to discover some form in which the modern consciousness in all its disruption and fragmentation can be represented. His problem is in part defined by the fact that his background was Dublin and his upbringing Jesuit. He was far more conscious than were English writers of a compact society, and he had been brought up in a world in which the recognition of sin was a reality. For him the break into the spiritual nihilism of the modern world was more violent and complete. The wound of that conflict is never absent entirely from his work. The past from which he departed was so compact and consolidated that his rupture from it leaves him lacerated beyond the hope of complete recovery. He seeks, like Eliot and Yeats, for some new mythology in which to express his awareness of the dilemma of modern man, and in *Ulysses* he achieves this without abandoning intelligibility. Like Eliot and Strachey, and other creative writers in the period, he looks upon the past with some strange mixture of nostalgia and contempt. To write thus is of course to simplify the issue. For though such thought does remain in Joyce's work, it is present rather as a sediment when the effect of his imagination is over. For his genius is sardonic and satiric, irreverent and comic, sensitive to every incongruity, and all this he uses, along with his musical gifts, to present his thought in such a new and captivating manner.

The outstanding originality of the volume lies in its employment of language. Joyce had a supremely sensitive ear and in his prose he mimics and parodies, and transcribes all the rhythms of speech from the colloquial to rhetoric. His language is indeed the most vital element in his contribution to form, and has an audacity and inventiveness unparalleled in English since Shakespeare. Unfortunately, unlike Shakespeare, he seldom used his linguistic genius for effects which are beautiful. His desire lay elsewhere, to break down the artificial barrier which syntax and rhetoric create between the written and the spoken speech, and between both of these and the record of thought in the mind. It is the gulf between the mind as it is, and the literary reproduction of its processes.

It is revealing that within this period there have been two very diverse attempts to investigate language. First C. K. Ogden in his *Basic English* attempts to make communication possible in 850 words, and secondly Joyce breaks up the whole concept of the word, as normally conceived, in order to present the mind in action. A significance must be attached to the fact that Ogden and Joyce were sympathetic with each other's attempts, and that Ogden was earlier than most of Joyce's contemporaries in realizing what he was endeavouring to do with the language. H. Levin has quoted the results obtained in 1937 by some American scholars directed by M. C. Hanley. They prepared a *Word Index to James Joyce's Ulysses*, and discovered that though *Ulysses* employs the resources of the language to the extent of 29,899 different words, over half of these appear only once, and many of the rest serve some special purpose that seldom requires them to be repeated. Almost half of the 260,430 words in the book are drawn from a basic vocabulary of about a hundred monosyllables, which closely coincide with the vocabulary of colloquial usage.

So to transmute language for his purposes was a task of supreme difficulty. He had first to assemble his material in the artificial but logical order of normal speech. This had a relationship to the ultimate text less close than an artist's first sketch to the final painting. For language, as ordinarily conceived, had to be translated into language as the image of the stream of consciousness. As has already been suggested, there were frequently added, as in Shakespeare, effects which come from wit and exuberance, but, in the main, all is concentrated on this central purpose of exposing a mind, caught for a day with other minds, in all the irrational associations and the swaying criss-cross of mental movements which we call life. The narrative has a temporal sequence and the successive stages of Bloom's day are necessary to the theme, yet so elaborate is the structure of reference from one phrase and incident to another that the whole seems almost without beginning or end. Begin it anywhere and you can continue to that point again; and have the completeness of all that Joyce wishes to convey. Anticipations and recollections make it on a first reading incomprehensible, for one must know all that comes after before the beginning is fully clear. It is as if, with all its complexity, the whole long narrative were one single image.

The element in Joyce which led to a scandal when the volume was first published was the sexual element, first in the use of some simple words, seldom seen on the printed page, though common enough in colloquial speech among certain sections of the community, and secondly some reference to sex of a character considered by the critics to be overbold. The presence of these elements cannot be denied, but as Judge John M. Woolsey stated in his admirable judgement in 1933, their effect is not pornographic : ' in many places the effect of *Ulysses* on the reader undoubtedly is somewhat emetic, nowhere does it tend to be an aphrodisiac.' Joyce is presenting sex to the degree which it can be assumed that it occupies the minds of his characters, and his vocabulary, as in other sections of his work, is an attempt to allow language to be no barrier between the reader and the exact presentation of truth. When everything is admitted, and when the fatuities of the attacks have been eliminated, it may yet be agreed that Joyce's mind dwelt more than that of many cultivated people amid the scatological sides of human life.

Despite all its great qualities, *Ulysses* lacks that universality of appeal which the greatest arts possess. There is a terrifying self-consciousness in the form, as if Joyce had lost faith in everything except his power to subdue words to his own use. He seems at times to use them, almost cruelly, as if he in his mastery over them avenged himself on life.

His strength and his weakness are well shown by Miss Rebecca West in *The Strange Necessity* (1928). Her essay is all the more revealing as it is obviously the recital of a profound personal experience on reading the book. She shows how Leopold Bloom is made with ' that peculiar squatting baseness which comes of a deliberate regression. His lack of dignity has the widest possible range, he travesties the whole nature of man.' She insists, more clearly than most of Joyce's critics, on his failure to represent any world outside that of Bloom's. It is his ' extraordinary incompetence ' which leads to his failure to show the elements in life through which man has been elevated, or any of the moments that have gestures of magnificence. Rebecca West is critical of all that is false in Joyce, his sentimentality, ugliness, and arrogant ostentation. At the same time she returns continually to the confession that the book contains something which she cannot escape, something which continually reasserts itself into her consciousness even when she would avoid it.

Many readers must have shared her experience. In that power of fixing attention on the vision of man in his baseness, Joyce has his greatness. In his failure equally to show how man has struggled against a sordid animalism lies his weakness and one-sidedness. The portrait of man's degradation might have lost its compelling strength if this balance in the vision had been maintained. He shows all the wild disordered degradation of which the mind is capable, but he fails to show the fight of the human spirit for orderliness and decency against all that jungle chaos. As Miss Rebecca West writes : ' I do most solemnly maintain that Leopold Bloom is one of the greatest creations of all time, that in him something true is said about man. Nothing happens to him at the end of *Ulysses*. Nothing is suggested in the course of the book which would reconcile him to the nobility of life. Simply he stands before us, convincing us that man wishes to fall back from humanity into earth, and that in that wish is power, as the façade of Notre-Dame stands above us convincing us that man wishes to rise from humanity into the sky, and that in that wish is power.'

The difficulty and complexity of *Ulysses* diminish into the category of minor problems when compared with those of *Finnegans Wake* (1939). Though it imaged all the irrationality of the conscious mind, *Ulysses* was still dealing mainly with the conscious mind and the objective world. *Finnegans Wake* is an attempt to achieve a similar exploration of the unconscious world of dream, and so to use language and symbols that all the bewildering inconsistencies and fantasies of a dream world can be represented. The longer the mind works upon *Ulysses* the clearer the narrative becomes and the more full of meaning, but endless toil devoted to *Finnegans Wake* could not induce the calm of order and reason into this verbal cauldron. For the aim of the whole is to present incoherence. Along with this is Joyce's use of the philosophy of Vico in *Scienza Nuova* that life is a perpetual cycle of change.

No critic will easily condemn the work of an honest and original artist for being incomprehensible without the greatest hesitation, for so often after a decade or a generation the difficulty disappears and the methods which were once revolutionary are accepted as part of a tradition. Yet *Finnegans Wake* does present some wholly exceptional features. The solution of its linguistic ingenuity would demand of the reader a very long period of research. Passages can indeed be read for the beauty of their sounds. Such for instance is the soliloquy of Anna Livia Plurabelle, the voice of the river Liffey (amnis Livia) with which the work closes. While in *Ulysses* the conventions of language have been broken and with great inventiveness, in order to create a new pattern of speech, in *Finnegans Wake* all pattern is destroyed. It is as if the author demanded that one should learn a new language in order to read his work, and to learn that language for this purpose only, accepting that each new word should exist once only in the unique place where its author has placed it. It is as if Joyce were at once nihilistic and totalitarian in his linguistic usage. Such procedure seems to have an arrogance of a supreme order, as if the exile were revenging himself on humanity. In its most violent manifestations it is a linguistic solipsism. This at least can be said, that *Ulysses* and *Finnegans Wake* are the end of a road. In the endeavour of using psycho-analysis in art, or of exploring the unconscious mind by linguistic means, no one can travel further. Joyce may not have many readers for *Finnegans Wake*, but the whole of his achievement in fiction has already had an influence and attracted a considerable critical attention.

CHAPTER V

D. H. LAWRENCE

WHATEVER may be the ultimate judgement on his work, D. H. Lawrence (1885-1930) is the most powerful personality within the period. He stands out among his contemporaries as one who lived intensely with a nature that was original, tempestuous, passionate. If elements in his life and work are to be described as a partial failure, they are only a failure because his achievement, if it is to be judged at all, must be judged by the standards of Shakespeare and Tolstoi. His work might have been more satisfactory had his talents been more varied, for his genius is undeniable. He is the first writer of proletarian origin in English literature who wins his way through to a life in which he can freely exercise his genius. When he gained his own identity he was unimpeded by convention and traditional conceptions. As a fiercely original mind he pursued his own path, and though sometimes this led into difficulty and obscurities, one is also conscious of some flame shining almost to the end with its first ardour unimpaired.

He was born in the mining village of Eastwood, near Nottingham, in one of a block of low brick cottages, with one window on the ground floor and one upstairs. Within a small, crowded house there was an intense clash of personalities which deeply affected his life. His father was a miner, rough, handsome, intemperate. His mother came of a family which bordered on the middle-classes, gentle, pious, a little puritanical. Their relation is well described by Middleton Murry in *Son of Woman* (1931), a study in which he states a strong case that

Lawrence's whole life was dependent on his devotion to his mother, and on the neurosis created by her influence over him. The importance of that influence can be allowed without accepting all that Murry has to say about it, nor need his other conclusions in this strange book be conceded while agreeing with this basic proposition from which they arise. In his largely autobiographical novel *Sons and Lovers*, Lawrence describes the conflict between the two : ' The pity was, she was too much his opposite. She could not be content with the little he might be; she would have him the much that he ought to be. So, in seeking to make him nobler than he could be, she destroyed him. She injured and hurt and scarred herself, but she lost none of her worth.'

In 1910 Lawrence's mother died, and in 1912 he began living with Frieda Weekley (*née* von Richtofen). They were married in 1914, and their strange, tense, tormented life continued until his death. Much of their early years were spent travelling in Europe, especially after the war of 1914-18, when Lawrence felt that England was spiritually exhausted. Later they visited Australia, which is the background of *Kangaroo*. Autobiographically this is one of the most important of the novels, for Lawrence also describes his life during the war when especially from 1916-18 he was subject to social and official persecution because of his German wife and his own indiscretions. Some of his later years were spent in New Mexico, where much that is best in his latest work was written. In 1930 he died of consumption in Vence. Though his main achievement is as a novelist, he was also a short-story writer of great power, and a poet. Above all he was a great letter-writer, and some will think that the letters can take their place with his novels as lively and original compositions in which the whole man is revealed.

In emphasizing the influence of Lawrence's mother, Murry probably under-estimated the importance of Frieda. She gave him the strength of a very powerful nature, and the confidence of an aristocratic tradition. Above all, she prevented him from dwindling from his proletarian origins into an ordinary bourgeois author. In another environment it is conceivable that, like others of his class, he might have followed the main stream of fiction so regularly and competently purveyed to the lending-library readers. Frieda was fiery, jealous, possessive, with a nature as strong as his own. Whatever their life may have been, a strange necessity linked them and kept them together. From the intensity of that life came the novels, the stories, the criticism and the poems, all the product of a nature which seemed on fire in some intense, unbreakable relation with another nature, not creative, but as powerful as his own.

Whatever may be its excesses, its eccentricity, and at times its unintelligible elements, Lawrence alone within the period discovers in the novels a view of life. Nor is this assimilated from reading, but caught fresh in life, from his own intuitions. Viewed from one point of view his novels are a long extended autobiography, in which though many of the scenes and characters are inverted, the spiritual and emotional life displayed is his own. He is the Rousseau of his age, dependent on feeling for the beginning of thought. In this he shows the anti-intellectualism so strong in the period, believing as he himself would say that all that was best began not in the brain but in the solar plexus. Late in his career he summarized his theories in three remarkable books, *Fantasia of the Unconscious* (1923); *Psychoanalysis and the Unconscious* (1923), and *Apocalypse* (1932). The theories have not been, however, imposed on his life, they are rather the conclusions of his keen but tormented existence. A contrast of his work with that of H. G. Wells shows the contrast between the two generations. For Wells has a mind which wanders over the whole of creation with an insatiable curiosity, ever seeking new knowledge and, except in his later years, confident that the mind can organize that knowledge for social purposes. Lawrence has ridden rough-shod past all this, with a romantic emotionalism, not unlike that of the Nazis which is grounded in irrationalism and is contemptuous of the achievements of knowledge and reason.

He began with a violent hatred for the ugly sordidness of industrial England as he had known it in his boyhood. The contrast between the drab helplessness of that world and the lively beauty of the countryside gave his picture of rural scenes, of animals, of the changes of season and the weather, a quality which is the most beautiful in all his work. The tender and close observation of those natural descriptions is already present in the early autobiographical novel *Sons and Lovers*, in 1913, and it is still there in *Lady Chatterley's Lover*, in 1931. This affection for nature owes its poignancy to the knowledge that close to the fields and the woods and the fresh air of the countryside, are the misshapen slag-heaps with their odours and ugliness, and an atmosphere dull and foul with smoke. The contrast is emphasized in many of his novels, as in the passage where he describes the Brangwens' farm, in *The Rainbow* : ' As they drove from town, the farmers of the land met the blackened colliers trooping from the pit-mouth. As they gathered the harvest, the west wind brought a faint sulphurous smell of pit-refuse burning. As they pulled the turnips in November the sharp clink-clink-clink-clink of empty trucks shunting on the line vibrated in their hearts with the fact of other activity going on beyond them.'

Out of that hatred of industrial England Lawrence reached a profound belief that in the crowded and inhibited life of modern cities the whole emotional and sexual life of man had been made mean and sordid. Expressed in its simplest form his desire was to restore to himself in his emotions the same liveliness and beauty as he had found in the countryside. To regard him as a philosopher or a teacher, as Middleton Murry does, is to limit and misunderstand his genius. As F. R. Leavis has written, he has affinities with Blake : ' He had the same gift of knowing what he was interested in, the same power of distinguishing his own feelings and emotions from conventional sentiment, the same " terrifying honesty ".' As Aldous Huxley, who knew and admired him so deeply, said, he was above all an artist with ' an extraordinary sensitiveness to what Wordsworth called " unknown modes of being ". He was always intensely aware of the mystery of the world, and the mystery was always for him a *numen*, divine. Lawrence could never forget, as most of us almost continuously forget, the drab presence of the otherness that lies beyond the boundaries of man's conscious mind. This special sensibility was accompanied by a prodigious power of rendering the immediately experienced otherness in terms of literary art.'

With such qualities it was inevitable that the sexual life should have for him a place of high importance. The audacity of his accounts of sexual experience. particularly in *The Rainbow* and *Lady Chatterley's Lover*, has often obscured the fact that he was not a sensualist, and that his mind was completely removed from prurience, libertinism or obscenity. Huxley recalls how shocked Lawrence was on reading the memoirs of Casanova, and at that time he was engaged on writing *Lady Chatterley's Lover*. He realized how small a place the conscious life of man, and particularly his intellectual life, occupies in relation to the whole of the life of the universe. At first sight it might appear that he must have reached such conclusions from a study of Freud and other psycho-analysts, but this is only a small part of the truth. Out of his own experience he perceives human existence as something which could be made active and lovely, and intuitive, but is surrounded by a universe which is hostile, powerful and concealed. In the sexual experience, when it occurs truly between man and woman that hostility between man and the great Unknown which surrounds him is momentarily resolved. It was as if sex had a mystical quality when man and woman were not merely instruments of passion, one to the other, but together in absolute union.

His ideas have some importance in themselves, for such a powerful protest illuminated the whole sordid furtiveness of the emotional life of men and women in the crowded industrial areas. Beyond its intrinsic importance Lawrence's statement of his philosophy and faith is valued as the basis from which his vision as a creative artist developed. Elements in that vision are to be regretted. His rejection of reason is always arbitrary and sometimes ill-tempered, and links him with the most unfortunate tendencies in European thought in his age. He was flung back upon an emotional individualism, at its best almost mystical, and at its worst mere egoism. Further, in excluding romanticism from man's emotional life, he lost much of grace and beauty. In compensation he has a strength of vision, and an awareness which no one else in his generation possessed. Had he belonged to the middle-class he would inevitably have inherited much from a cultural tradition. As it was his proletarian origins led him to make his whole spiritual life out of his own experiences.

It is interesting to know how his mind would have developed had it not been for the lacerating effects of his unusual experiences in the war of 1914-18. Ill-health made him a non-combatant, but he felt the isolation of his position, and this was accentuated by the attention of petty persecution of the authorities arising from his own reputation and the nationality of his wife. The change can be seen by contrasting *Sons and Lovers* (1913), a full and vivid autobiographical novel, and *Kangaroo* (1923), which shows not only a deeply wounded personality but a despair for modern Western civilization itself. Such a conclusion was perhaps inevitable, but without the war it might not have come in such a hurt and precipitous way. His antagonism was accentuated by the banning in 1915 of *The Rainbow*, a novel to which he had devoted three years of close toil. It was this sense of frustration and hatred that sent him voyaging to Australia and to New Mexico, searching for some society where he could have a warm and fully moving life without the cerebral itch and the sense of responsibility for what had come to seem a sordid and corrupt civilization. As long as he was in England he felt responsible, for as Huxley points out, he confessed that he felt himself English in the teeth of all the world, even in the teeth of England.

Middleton Murry in *Son of Woman* suggests that Lawrence collapsed in his middle and later work. Such a view is only tenable if one accepts the grotesque conception which Murry has created of Lawrence as a failed messiah. Once one realizes with Huxley that Lawrence is primarily an artist, then the range and vital originality of this mature work becomes immediately apparent. In *Aaron's Rod* (1922) and *The Woman Who Rode Away* (1928) he shows his power of portraying emotion and passion between man and woman, and also of friendships between men. Both here and in *The Plumed Serpent* (1926), where he seeks release in primitive Mexican society, it can be argued that his highly individual experience and the thought which emerged from it have an excessive place. But apart from all this he has widened the whole conception of how the emotional and sexual life can be described in words. He has achieved something for that inner emotional and passionate part of man, as Wordsworth in his nature description attained a revelation of a range of sensibility previously unconceived. Much of this is contrived with great tenderness, which seems to parallel that gentle insight Lawrence possessed into the lives of animals, and into the scenes of nature. It is inevitable that harsher and even more cruel moments should enter, and indeed the picture would be very incomplete without them.

For Murry the final collapse of Lawrence is in *Lady Chatterley's Lover* (1931), a novel which gained notoriety on first publication for the frankness of its sexual descriptions. Murry's view may be summarized in the following passages : ' In *Lady Chatterley's Lover* sex blots out the universe. The great religious and creative purpose which, according to the *Fantasia*, a

E

man must have and to which he must be obedient even to the gates of hell, in order that there should be a true relation between man and woman—this great purpose has wholly disappeared. There is only one purpose in life, and it is the sexual act. The sexual act is all in all, and the great creative purpose has dwindled, in Lawrence, to the writing of the most detailed celebration of the sexual act the English language has known, or is likely to know again.' This is an excessive judgement, and in pursuit of a theory about Lawrence's mind, ignores what was great in his artistic achievement.

It is true that Lawrence had been wounded by the several attacks which had described his work as pornographic. To an artist who had such integrity, who revised and rewrote with such unremitting care, such charges must have been hard to bear. At moments he may have weakened, and felt that he would give his audience what it had seemed to expect from him. Also in periods of irritation he wrote and said things about his work and his intentions which he would not have confirmed in his more serious moments. Nor does the work itself substantiate these comments. Further, in these later years his health was bad, and this had created in him a loneliness and a bitter quality which contrasted with the vitality of the middle years. His search throughout his long travels, for some more primitive civilization where he could be quiescent and yet strong, had failed. He returns in on himself to England, and to the scenes of his own early life. All these motives appear in *Lady Chatterley's Lover*. The more theatrical passages of the other novels of the middle and later period largely disappear. For this reason those who think of Lawrence as a philosopher may find it less profound and original than some of his works. But it has beauty and tenderness. It has the strange sadness of one who has struggled long and illuminated much in life, but never found completeness, and who now knows that death waits in attendance.

Lawrence could write with bitterness during those last years,

but that the spirit of tenderness is not dead can be seen in
the strangely beautiful story of *The Man Who Died* (1931).
Written with great simplicity is a story of a resurrected Jesus,
who came to know of human love. The theme is one which
many will obviously condemn as in itself improper. Yet it
would be difficult for any reader to discover irreverence in the
treatment. All theory and discussion are excluded, and one
feels that Lawrence is seeking through the very narrative itself
some union between the love that is in Christianity and that
other love of the human body passionate and yet quiescent. In
that love some knowledge is obtained by men of each other
and some union with that other world, outside self, is obtained.

CHAPTER VI

ALDOUS HUXLEY

IN all the earlier stages of his work Aldous Huxley is the writer most representative of the generations who lived between the wars. Others may have a greater creative power, D. H. Lawrence, Yeats, and Joyce, but no one was so aware of the ultimate problems of the time or approached them with such a wide equipment of knowledge and understanding. His novels and criticism are a mirror in which the age could perceive itself with its shifting hopes and disillusionments, the changes from the harsh gaiety of the twenties to the solemn acceptance of the thirties that tragedy is approaching. More than any other writer of that time he had an instructed appreciation of the other arts, of painting and particularly of music. His attempt in *Point Counter Point* at a 'musicalization' of fiction was based on a profound knowledge of both arts. Further, he, more than any of his contemporaries, had the equipment to construct some bridge between science and the arts in an age when those two great aspects of human activity were so unhappily divided.

He was born in 1894 and the sciences and the arts were parts of his family inheritance. His grandfather was T. H. Huxley the defender of Darwin in the controversies over evolution. His father, Leonard Huxley, was a Professor of Greek and editor of *The Cornhill*, and his mother was related to Matthew Arnold. Environment and education confirmed these hereditary advantages. At Eton and Balliol he was distinguished as a scholar, and soon his independent and critical mind expanded towards creative work. During his youth he suffered

58

a period of partial blindness which was obviously a profound experience. It must have emphasized that solitary element in his temperament which becomes strongly apparent in the mysticism of his later work. It may have developed also that bitter and frustrated mood which often appears in his writing. His earliest publications were in verse : *The Burning Wheel* (1916) and *The Defeat of Youth* (1918). These volumes had a romantic and idealistic quality which disappeared in his later work.

Of his contemporaries D. H. Lawrence alone had any considerable influence on Huxley, and his admiration is well expressed in a preface to his edition of Lawrence's letters. The two seemed in every way contrasted. Lawrence, the miner's son, is largely self-educated, and deprived of any traditional background which he can inherit and exploit, he has to discover everything for himself. Huxley, on the other hand, seems often overweighted with knowledge, his own creative ability struggling to independence through accumulations of learning. Lawrence is like some spirit on fire whose passion and intensity know neither rest nor abatement, while Huxley has a cerebral emphasis, critical and sardonic which has a debilitating influence on his emotions.

It was in the post-war period in 1920 that he first discovered his own individual talent with *Limbo*, a volume of short stories. *Crome Yellow*, the first of the novels, followed in 1921, and *Antic Hay* in 1923. *Crome Yellow* has a mood of light-hearted comedy in its satire, and it is rather with *Antic Hay*, a daring and original volume, that Huxley first established himself as a new force in English fiction. The mood of the novel was implied by the quotation from Marlowe on the title page :

> My men like satyrs grazing on the lawns
> Shall with their goat-feet dance the antic hay.

He exposes the bitter disillusionment of post-war England

with its accompanying moral recklessness, and in a mixture of satire and comedy he displays this world with a bitter delight. Part of the boldness was a verbal exuberance not without a certain pleasure derived from a consciousness that the volume would shock many readers. Huxley, like Rimbaud, would seem to wish to avenge himself on a society whose compact stupidity he deplored. It was this liveliness, unrestrained in its desperate gaiety, that gave the volume much of its attractiveness to the post-war generation. Yet there strayed through this coruscation of wit moments suggestive of more profound thought, with poignant gestures almost of pity for the present fate of humanity. Sometimes the wit and the thought would become entangled so that the seriousness and the macabre comedy united.

A disillusionment, which is almost unalleviated, clings around the volume and seems to symbolize the world of a generation that had lost all hope in the future. So in one of the passages which approaches 'essay' material, Gumbril senior explaining how men refuse to benefit by experience illustrates his theme with an example from the life of Sir Christopher Wren : ' He offered them open spaces and broad streets; he offered them sunlight and air and cleanliness; he offered them beauty, order and grandeur. He offered to build for the imagination and the ambitious spirit of man, so that even the most bestial, vaguely and remotely, as they walked those streets might feel that they were of the same race—or very nearly—as Michelangelo; that they too might feel themselves, in spirit at least, magnificent, strong, and free. He offered them all these things; he drew a plan for them, walking in peril among the still smouldering ruins. But they preferred to re-erect the old intricate squalor; they preferred the medieval darkness and crookedness and beastly irregular quaintness; they preferred holes and crannies and winding tunnels; they preferred foul smells, sunless, stagnant air, phthisis and rickets; they preferred ugliness and pettiness and dirt; they preferred the wretched human scale, the scale of the sickly body not of the mind.'

The comment in that passage, though penetrating, has a basis of normality. But Huxley often exposes his disillusionment with the world in an atmosphere where bitterness, desiring to revenge itself on life, calls in elements that deliberately befoul all that is normally held in reverence or esteem. One of the most illuminating passages of this type in *Antic Hay* is in the conversation of one of the characters named Coleman : ' I remember, when I used to hang about the biological laboratories at school, eviscerating frogs—crucified with pins, they were, belly upwards, like little green Christs—I remember once, when I was sitting there, quietly poring over the entrails, in came the laboratory boy and said to the stinks usher : " Please, sir, may I have the key of the Absolute ? " And, would you believe it, that usher calmly put his hand in his trouser pocket and fished out a small Yale key and gave it him without a word. What a gesture ! The key of the Absolute. But it was only the absolute alcohol the urchin wanted—to pickle some loathsome foetus in, I suppose. God rot his soul in peace ! '

All of the early Huxley, in his strength and weakness, is in that passage. It is significant that the background is biological, the theme ultimately religion and mysticism however profanely approached, while staring out of the passage, ugly and lacerated, is this strange sense that the human body in its generation and functioning is foul and contemptible. It was as if Jonathan Swift had studied science and had abandoned all hope in the Christian faith, but had preserved in a heightened form his disgust with the animal aspect of man's life.

Those Barren Leaves followed in 1925, and with it a change can be perceived in Huxley's outlook. Technically the novel shows little development, for as in *Crome Yellow* the emphasis is on conversation, much in the manner of Peacock. It has no form or plot beyond the creation of opportunities for discussion. Its purpose is more serious than that in *Crome Yellow*, and for this very reason some of the conversation is dull. Struggling for definition without complete success there is an element at once more philosophical and serious than anything which has appeared in the earlier volumes. Huxley would appear, a little in advance of his generation, to be rejecting, or at least modifying, the reckless and despairing wit and the enforced, sometimes inebriated gaiety, of the early twenties. His concern with morality becomes positive, and with his interest in the good life there emerges a preoccupation with mysticism. It is this extension of vision which gives the novel its mental uncertainty and technical insecurity.

Often in the life of a creative writer there occurs the desire to seek differently and more deeply into the experience which life offers for investigation. The resulting necessity for a change in form leads often to a temporary maladjustment in the design achieved. So it is with Huxley in *Those Barren Leaves*, as it is with Shakespeare in *King John*, where in each work an imperfection in actual performance arises from a newly quickened creative curiosity. Apart from the mystical elements Huxley allows at times a tender and almost sentimental quality to intrude, though some other side of his nature watches this with a cynical and distrustful eye. *Those Barren Leaves* is a novel in which Huxley is redefining his position, and the restlessness of mood, and the inadequacy at times in style and form are resolved in the works which follow. For he proceeds in the same seriousness of mood, though with greater confidence, to *Point Counter Point* (1928), and to *Eyeless in Gaza* (1936).

Point Counter Point is Huxley's greatest achievement in the novel. He has composed a narrative in which the emphasis is not on plot as ordinarily conceived, nor even on character, as character is portrayed in the development of a story. He has discovered a form through which the whole image of a society can be conveyed, and in so doing he has developed far from the satire and conversation in the manner of Peacock and Meredith which he employed in the earlier novels. His aim is probably best described by the reflections of Philip Quarles on fiction in *Point Counter Point*. Quarles discusses the ' musicalization ' of fiction not ' in the symbolist way, by subordinating sense to sound ', but in the construction itself. In Beethoven ' a theme is started, then developed, pushed out of shape, imperceptibly deformed, until, though still recognizably the same, it has become quite different'. The novelist can achieve a similar effect in several ways, he can have abrupt transitions with an amplitude of characters and 'parallel, contrapuntal plots'; he can modulate by reduplicating situations and characters or confronting similar people with dissimilar situations. Further, 'the novelist can assume the godlike creative privilege and simply elect to consider the events of the story in their various aspects—emotional, scientific, economic, religious, metaphysical, etc. He will modulate from one to the other—as from the aesthetic to the physico-chemical aspect of things, from the religious to the physiological or financial.'

Such methods are employed to produce a ruthless exposure of modern society, and beyond that, a presentation of man as the helpless victim of his own biological limitations. All romance is dead, and the spiritual is a fantasy. Even consciousness seems some itch, trivial, irritating, only some excrescence, temporary, perhaps affecting the animal life of man. In some ways the conclusions though reached by a different passage of thought are like those of Eliot in *The Waste Land*, for they both present a sense of helplessness and disillusionment. Huxley's reflections have been guided by a fuller study of science with an emphasis on the biological control over life, compared with which he would seem to suggest that the mind, and indeed the whole conscious life, are trivial and transitory.

The biological origin seems to haunt him, making reverence impossible and robbing all life of magnificence. As he writes at the opening of *Point Counter Point*, ' what had been a blob of jelly within her body would invent a god and worship '. Despite his grim analysis of life, and adding poignancy to its ugly outline, Huxley shows a keen and sensitive interest in art and music, in literature and verse. Yet the enjoyment of these pleasures is never allowed completely to obscure his knowledge of the helplessness of man : ' What had blindly lived in her as a parasitic worm would look at the stars, would listen to music, would read poetry.'

Throughout the novel there has been a concentration on the portrayal of the sexual life which is almost a preoccupation. It was as if somehow Huxley, like Swift, found the body an instrument foul and obscene, whose operations he could not contemplate without horror. Yet his nature will not permit him to withdraw his mind from this physical side of life. He is forced to image it, and he prefigures in his imagination all that is most detestable in its detail when regarded with a cold objectivity that seems compounded of the morbid and the clinical. It is true that the only happy characters he presents are figures like Lucy Tantamount, who are frank sensualists, without any illusions about the value of mental or spiritual activities. But Huxley is powerless either to accept their view or to cease contemplating it with his imagination. Mind may be a fantasy, but it is a fantasy which wrecks the animal man, and turns him into a complex and dissatisfied dichotomy divided against himself and often intricate in the devices with which he indulges in his uncleanliness. The same thought led to his satire experiment, *Brave New World* in 1932, which shows a society in which the reactions of the members are automatically controlled.

In 1938 came *Ends and Means* where Huxley abandons fiction and gives a simple and direct presentation of his thought. Like all the most sensitive minds of his generation he felt keenly the terrible disintegration in Europe in the decade between 1928 and 1938. He was determined to state his faith and in some way indicate a solution before it was too late. The degree of his seriousness can be seen in the fact that he has abandoned the wit, and all the surface cleverness of the novels, to state his thoughts as simply as possible. Often he carries out this aim so thoroughly that in prose style some of the passages are lumpish and dull.

It is in this volume that he first gives coherent statement to the mystical faith which found some expression in *Those Barren Leaves* and *Eyeless in Gaza*. He is concerned with the major world problems which in 1938 had become so tragically imminent, the problem of war and peace, and the whole question of the freedom and integrity of the individual.

The volume was not only an analysis of the contemporary inadequacy of life, it was a severely practical attempt at reform, beginning with the individual life, and considering further how increased influence could be gained by groups of individuals who had reached a similar conviction. It is difficult briefly to describe this faith. Huxley, himself, defines it as ' non-attachment '. ' The ideal man is the non-attached man. Non-attached to his bodily sensations and lusts. Non-attached to his cravings for power and possessions. Non-attached to the objects of these various desires. Non-attached to his anger and hatred; non-attached to his exclusive loves. Non-attached to wealth, fame, social position. Non-attached even to science, art, speculation, philanthropy.' He was already indicating the permanent elements in the great faiths of the world, and this he was to emphasize later in *The Perennial Philosophy*. The main sources of the conception of ' non-attachment ' lay for him in the great religions of the Far East: ' We find it (along with everything else!) in Hinduism. It is at the very heart of the teachings of the Buddha. For the Chinese the doctrine is formulated by Lao Tsu.' While he finds ample evidence of this mystical faith among Christian philosophers his attitude is hardening against organized and official Christianity as such with its extremes from ' extravagant asceticism to the most brutally cynical forms of *realpolitik* '.

So in *Ends and Means*, in the year before barbarism was to spread over Europe, Huxley, made serious by the portents of what lay ahead, preached the good life, of active chastity, of courage and charity, and of the annihilation of selfishness. The doctrine came too late, and from this volume onwards Huxley's influence as a writer, imaging the mood of his generation, steadily declines. For Europe, instead of exercising ' non-attachment ', chose war, chaos, and the ultimate barbarisms. But though his influence has diminished, it may well be that later, when men try again to rediscover the road to sanity, they will turn for guidance to *Ends and Means*.

Of the work which he has produced since the outbreak of the war the most notable is *Grey Eminence* (1941), the biography of the Capuchin monk who began as a mystic and ended as Richelieu's adviser during the barbarism of the Thirty Years War. Huxley is fully aware of contemporary parallels, and in this sombre picture it would seem that his distrust of human life is gaining emphasis in this seventeenth-century illustration of the way the life of the contemplative is corrupted by the world of action.

The years of the second world war have found Huxley in the United States where he had already settled before the catastrophe was upon us. It can without injustice be said that his influence has diminished and that the European who comes to his later books finds in them no awareness of his immediate and urgent problems. *The Perennial Philosophy* (1946) is his elaborate restatement of the mystical philosophy which he had first defined as ' non-attachment '. To Christendom his hostility would seem to have increased, and so one who began as being so representative of his age, seems at present an isolated figure, but one whose mind remains supremely sensitive and interesting. Yet no one who has lived through the mental life of these decades can honestly fail to recognize how wide his influence has been. He was a figure symbolical of his generation, as H. G. Wells had represented an earlier and more confident age.

CHAPTER VII

VIRGINIA WOOLF

THE work of Virginia Woolf covers the whole period under review. Her first volume, *The Voyage Out*, was published in 1915 and her last, *Between the Acts*, in 1941, while her tragic death in that year seemed the end of an age. It marks the close as it were, for the time being, of liberalism in England with all the best of its intellectual and imaginative inheritance. She was the daughter of Leslie Stephen, a critic and historian of great culture and taste, who had left Cambridge to pursue writing as a career because his agnosticism would not permit him to conform to the requirements of the University. He was the child of that cultural world which existed exclusively in those later nineteenth-century decades, where a rejection of the Christian faith had given the mind an increased liberty while leaving as yet unimpaired the practical ethics on which society and the individual life had been based as a result of centuries of Christian tradition.

There was a hollowness in that world, for it derived its strength from a spiritual tradition from which it had consciously and indeed elaborately disinherited itself, but the loss was not yet apparent. This atmosphere of learned and intellectual freedom Virginia Woolf inherited. She moved in circles where in discussion and controversy there were no taboos, and, unlike some of her predecessors as women writers, she surveyed with a mind totally unabashed the perversions and cruelties of life. Often she knew these things with her mind only, as if her own personality, delicate and never overstrong, held itself in reserve. Similarly her nature had elements which were gay and romantic, admiring the Elizabethan voyagers, and the adventurers in strange countries, though again she seemed to survey all this with a self-withholding quiescence. In part it is the consciousness that she was a woman, and that society had excluded women from so many places of pleasure and privilege, from the great offices of the State to the High Tables of Cambridge Colleges. In *A Room of One's Own* she gives a poignant picture of what would have been the fate of a sister of Shakespeare's in Elizabethan London.

Further, as became known after her suicide, the mind which contained her sensitive imaginings had been even more delicate and fragile than was generally realized. Already in the war of 1914-18 she had been affected by moods of acute depression, one of which had led to a serious though temporary breakdown. Often the tasks of writing would produce neurasthenic conditions which led to sensations of blank despair, and the fear of insanity dogged her. It is not difficult to imagine how the outbreak of the second world war would affect her. Her home had been destroyed by enemy action and she was exhausted with the writing of *Between the Acts*. Death and the movements of water are both often to be found in her novels. So she died by drowning in the River Ouse. ' I feel certain ', she wrote in the note that Leonard Woolf, her husband, found after her death, ' that I am going mad again. I feel we can't go through another of those terrible times. And I shan't recover this time.'

In the novel she developed her own technique, consciously working out from the realism of Arnold Bennett and his contemporaries to effects which were similar to those of the French impressionists whose work she knew so well. In a paper entitled *Mr. Bennett and Mrs. Brown*, delivered to the ' Heretics ' Society at Cambridge in 1924, she challenged the whole basis of Edwardian realism by asking how those novelists would have portrayed ' Mrs. Brown '. She suggested that they would ' begin by saying that her father kept a shop in Harro-

gate. Ascertain the rent. Ascertain the wages of the shop
assistants in the year 1879. Discover what the mother died
of. Describe cancer. Describe calico. Describe. But I cried
" Stop! Stop! " And I regret to say that I threw that ugly,
that clumsy, that incongruous tool out of the window.'

She knew that if she was to rely on realistic description the
vision she had of Mrs. Brown ' would have been dulled and
tarnished and vanished for ever '. Plot, she reduced to a minimum, and description, as conceived by the realistic novelist,
she eliminated. Like the great liberal which at heart she was,
her concentration lay on character, and character she brought
to life not through a series of logically ordered incidents but
by touches of detail, so that records of thought, associations,
and references to past experience all worked into a unified
portrait that had a poetic quality.

Her contribution to form in the novel is described in a
volume by Winifred Holtby which, despite some effective later
criticism, remains one of the most lively studies. Winifred
Holtby comments on the great liberties which Virginia Woolf
had taken with the conventions : ' She had thrown overboard
much that had been commonly considered indispensable to
the novel, descriptions of places, and families, explanations
of environment, a plot of external action, dramatic scenes,
climaxes, conclusions, and almost all those link sentences which
bind one episode to the next. But much remained to her.
She had retained her preoccupation with life and death, with
character, and with the effect of characters grouped and inter-
acting. She had kept her consciousness of time and movement.
She knew how present and past are interwoven, and how to-day
depends so much upon knowledge and memory of yesterday,
and fear or confidences in to-morrow. She was still preoccupied
with moral values; she was immensely excited about form and
the way in which the patterns of life grow more and more
complex as one regards them.'

Virginia Woolf's descriptions of her own methods in fiction

are admirable. At the same time it would be undesirable if younger writers regarded her comments as having any permanent validity. It would indeed be unhappy if the novel lost background, and description and realism in which so many of its great triumphs have been won. One can only emphasize again that the artists in this period had special problems, faced as they were with a fragmentation of society and a disruption in civilization. They were led into strange paths, and so in a never fully satisfactory way they recover something of that spiritual element in life which the materialism of the previous generation had subdued. There still remains, however, the great and comprehensive tradition of Shakespeare, and Balzac, and Dickens.

It is possible to discover a development in her work and in her experiments with form. The earliest novel, *The Voyage Out* (1915), retains a plot, though not a very striking one. Superficially the story centres on a young girl, who has not reached maturity. Her development is shown until she dies of fever soon after she has fallen in love. Already it is characterization rather than the story which occupies her, and her plot is only the mental world in which her people live. *Night and Day* followed in 1919 with a clearly defined theme, in which a clever and cultured young woman rejects one lover and accepts another. In the heroine there are some autobiographical elements. The whole work is far more elaborate than this brief narration of the central theme would suggest. It was with *Jacob's Room* (1922) that she came to maturity. In some ways this is Virginia Woolf's novel about the war of 1914-18, for the theme centres upon the life of Jacob from his childhood to his days in Cambridge and his youthful years, to his death in the war. With more confidence than in the earlier novels she has employed the theme for the portrayal of mental atmosphere which becomes her major purpose in novel writing. *Mrs. Dalloway* followed in 1925, the most clearly defined of all her works and one of the most satisfactory. The

F

time covered in that novel by the external action, such as it is, occupies only twelve hours, from the morning when Mrs. Dalloway goes out to buy her flowers for her party to the evening when the party is over. But the psychological method permits the whole of life to be shown in between. The entire existence of the single personality in the interval between birth and death is shown in that civilization of which we have now almost lost sight, where the life of the single personality is of such supreme importance. In that world an indulgence in personal emotions was not only permissible, but was indeed the main preoccupation of the cultured life.

Two years later, in 1927, she published *To the Lighthouse*, which some have regarded as the most poetical and satisfactory of her works. She reduced the externals of plot description to a minimum as if she had won her freedom completely from the tradition of realism. The group of characters presented have a close relation one to the other, so that the novel as a whole is a symbol of time and life and death. In 1931 she published *The Waves*, a novel which excluded plot as commonly understood altogether. It was as if she were writing a prose poem, in which her six characters gave through their own monologues their self-conscious knowledge of their own lives from birth onwards. The form was difficult to maintain and not wholly successful, but it is a new adventure in creative writing and the skill of her prose is nowhere better shown than in the way in which she differentiates one character from the other.

It was six years before her next novel, *The Years*, appeared in 1937. She seemed here to be reverting to a simpler form in showing the life of a family over a number of years. Yet this is no description or presentation of the social scene in any ordinary sense. Virginia Woolf had not entered into competition with Galsworthy. She was rather attempting to use her own individual conception of experience as a perpetual flow united by moments of retrospect and anticipation. It may be that the novel does not build up to a synthesis such as is achieved in *Mrs. Dalloway* or *To the Lighthouse*. The quality of the individual passages remains and the vision of the multiple movement of life at any given moment.

Her final novel, *Between the Acts*, of 1941, was an unfinished work, but one of great brilliance and charm and new promise. In this record of Virginia Woolf's work I have so far omitted any reference to *Orlando*, the imaginary biography based on the life of Victoria Sackville-West and published in 1928. The most acute of all Virginia Woolf's critics, Mrs. Joan Bennett, writing on her work as a novelist excludes *Orlando* and indeed does not list it among the novels. If it is not a novel it is difficult to know how this work is to be described, and to my mind its omission makes the interpretation of the place of *Between the Acts* in Virginia Woolf's development altogether impossible.

Orlando is the most gay, fantastic, light-hearted of all Virginia Woolf's achievements. The elements which are absent or suppressed in the rest of her work here gain an amplitude of expression. The colour and romantic sensibility to which she is obviously attached is in this work lavishly employed. Time which occupies her in the other novels is enlisted as part of the fantasy in *Orlando*, for the character who is a youth at the close of the Elizabethan period lives on in one guise or another through the centuries to be a woman in 1928. It is true that the work is set out as an imaginary biography, and that some details and portraits connect it with the life of Miss Sackville-West who was Mrs. Virginia Woolf's friend. All this is, however, only part of the fantasy on which the novel is based.

Nowhere else in the novels has the prose the same brilliance, as for instance in Virginia Woolf's description of the great frost in the early seventeenth century, of which the following is only a brief part of a most notable passage : ' The Court was at Greenwich, and the new King seized the opportunity that his coronation gave him to curry favour with the citizens. He directed that the river, which was frozen to a depth of twenty feet or more for six or seven miles on either side, should be swept, decorated and given all the semblance of a park or pleasure ground, with arbours, mazes, alleys, drinking booths, etc., at his expense. For himself and the courtiers, he reserved a certain space immediately opposite the Palace gates; which, railed off from the public only by a silken rope, became at once the centre of the most brilliant society in England. Great statesmen, in their beards and ruffs, despatched affairs of state under the crimson awning of the Royal Pagoda.' If only the exuberance of that passage could have entered her other work, uniting itself with a physical vitality which gave her a zest for all types of experience, she would have become one of the greatest of English novelists.

In *Orlando*, as she extends her imagination from contemporary, upper middle-class society, back across the centuries to Elizabethan days, she seems to gain a release of that physical energy so frequently absent in her novels. At the same time *Orlando* misses the profundity of vision which the other novels possess. Instead of the mystery of life and death there is wit, and irony. The greatness of *Between the Acts* is that here she seemed to be feeling her way to a combination of the historical pageantry and colour of *Orlando* and the insight of the novels. Incomplete as the novel is, it had the promise that she was about to stretch out into some enlargement of her interpretation of life. Instead, she died.

CHAPTER VIII

THE NEW BIOGRAPHY

THROUGHOUT the whole period there has been an
attack on man as an instrument for the civilized life, an
increasing satire on his emotional and sexual life, a mocking
of his idealism and a cynical emphasis on his inadequacy to
control the problems with which destiny faces him. Already
during the earlier years of the century G. B. Shaw had been
conducting a warfare against romanticism in which comedy
had been his main weapon. Each cherished idol was in turn
exposed. In the settled atmosphere of that first decade of the
century the attack did not seem severe or particularly profound
or urgent. Rather the comedy was enjoyed as a game of para-
dox, and the dramatist regarded as a jester whom such a well-
established society could easily afford. So the audiences who
first saw the exposure of the romantic conception of the soldier
in *Arms and the Man* thought in the terms of entertainment
remote from the reality of war. The play gained a very different welcome in its revival after 1918 by an audience who
appreciated the comedy far more fully because they knew what
soldiering really implied.

Shaw's criticism had been written from a background of
economic and social security, but a later generation was to
look out on some of these problems with more uncertain eyes.
There developed, for instance, in the later years of the war,
and there continued into the post-war period, an increasing
absence of confidence in man's capacity to control his own
future. One of the most brilliant, though sinister, exercises
in this satiric portraiture was to be found in J. M. Keynes's

The Economic Consequences of the Peace (1919), a volume which for meritorious intentions and disastrous results is outstanding in the period. In a few brief phrases he described the leaders of the Great Powers at their work of preparing the Treaty of Versailles. The public reputation of these world figures is pierced by his wit which would be pure entertainment did not the reader also contemplate that if these summaries were sober estimates then leadership in the modern world was indeed bankrupt. So Keynes wrote of President Wilson : ' But in fact the President had thought out nothing; when it came to practice, his ideas were nebulous and incomplete. He had no plan, no scheme, no constructive ideas whatever for clothing with the flesh of life the commandments which he had thundered from the White House. He could have preached a sermon on any of them or have addressed a stately prayer to the Almighty for their fulfilment; but he could not frame their concrete application to the actual state of Europe.' Not less brilliant but unhopeful was the picture which he gave of the Council as a whole : ' My last and most vivid impression is of such a scene—the President and the Prime Minister as the centre of a surging mob and a babel of sound, a welter of eager, impromptu compromises and counterproposals, all sound and fury signifying nothing, on what was an unreal question anyway, the great issues of the morning's meeting forgotten and neglected; and Clemenceau, silent and aloof on the outskirts—for nothing which touched the security of France was forward—throned, in grey gloves, on the brocade chair, dry in soul and empty of hope, very old and tired, but surveying the scene with a cynical and almost impish air.'

Those phrases of the dryness of soul, the emptiness of hope, the tiredness, and the cynical impishness seemed to symbolize so much in the period. Nor was the age content only with indicating the inadequacy of its own leaders, for it turned upon the past, and as if to prove that its own dilemma was permanent in the history of mankind, it set almost systematically to prove that the great ones of the past, the heroes and the leaders and the prophets, had never existed but were an illusion of an admiring but uncritical multitude.

It may not have been accidental that among the many literary friends of Lord Keynes was Lytton Strachey (1880-1932). In the years before the war he had mainly been known for a volume of criticism, *Landmarks in French Literature* (1912), which though it had wit, and great critical power, gave only minor indications of the later development of his genius. It witnessed clearly his indebtedness to French writers, and the delights which he shared with them in an attachment to lucidity and a fastidious gaiety. It is appropriate that some of his most successful comments are made on Voltaire, and in his portrait of the great French satirist one sees the outline of some of his later methods in description : ' His long, gaunt body, frantically gesticulating, his skull-like face, with its mobile features twisted into an eternal grin, its piercing eyes sparkling and darting—all this suggested the appearance of a corpse galvanized into an incredible animation.' Already Strachey was developing in his own mind, though it may not yet have been apparent to his readers, what Clifford Bower-Shore has well called ' the agnosticism of biography '.

In 1918, the concluding year of the war, there appeared *Eminent Victorians* which initiated a new period in English biography. The adjective ' Eminent ' was employed with a deliberately satirical intention, for in his portraits of Manning, Thomas Arnold, Florence Nightingale, and Gordon of Khartoum he sought to show that the public reputation with which the Victorians enshrined their heroes was apt to disguise the real personality, odd, incongruous, sometimes mean, often comic and of a stature strangely diminished from the gigantesque and solemn shapes that appeared in public on official occasions.

Against the whole tradition of Victorian biography with its

emphasis on the virtues, and its conscious concealment of all that did not contribute to that conception, Strachey was in revolt. His ironic talents, finding an additional emphasis by their identity with the spirit of the age, led him to carry these attacks very far, so that justice is obscured at times by the requirements of satire. It was as if in destroying the Victorian formula he had preceded with such vigour that he had inverted it, and left only the shortcomings of his victims exposed. The spirit which dwells behind Strachey's writing is, however, not a satiric one in this merely destructive sense. With Swift, a writer to whom he has many parallels, he shares a certain complexity of mind. A hidden sense of beauty dwells with him even when he is satirizing the ugliness of life, and tenderness is ever near, ready to enter at the least beckoning. As his early work shows and as his latest volume, *Elizabeth and Essex* (1928), reaffirms he possessed a latent romantic quality, and a very sensitive appreciation of beauty. Further, he seemed even in his malicious moments to have a concealed desire for a more honest view of life, freer and more genuine in its relationships where all the pretentiousness of the great, and all the pomp by which dwarfs were made into giants, had disappeared.

It can be conceded that there was a certain danger in his *Eminent Victorians* that his biographical method should degenerate into a formula, and indeed in the hands of some of his imitators it became only too apparent how facilely, and with what disastrous effects such a declension could occur. The author would select some figure of well-established renown, and then discovering a whole series of incongruous aspects and characteristics would unite them in a single portrait. Strachey himself seemed to have discovered in *Queen Victoria* a subject predestined by Providence for such treatment. On the one hand, there was the Empress with her vast territories, and the pomp that must inevitably surround an imperial court. On the other hand, there was the Queen herself, as she appeared in her own person, diminutive, ample, unshapely, dressed shabbily, almost humbly in her widow's weeds. The effect of the treatment of such a theme in the manner of the *Eminent Victorians* seemed obvious, but the obvious did not happen. A struggle develops in the volume between the Queen and Lytton Strachey and the Queen wins. Indeed after the death of the Prince Consort he struggles no longer, and is ultimately at hand to console the ageing monarch. The quality of the study is enhanced by this element of tenderness and the reader accepts it all readily because it is unexpected.

The exposure of the past was the element in Strachey's biographical method which was most imitated. Previously the biographer had been content to look up to the subject of his study, but now, instead, from some height in an empyrean of malice he looked down on the dwarf who straddles across the human scene in comic incongruity, masquerading in the trappings of a giant. Throughout the period this type of biography remains. It fitted into the taste of the time and seemed indeed one of the ways in which a bewildered and unhappy generation revenged itself on the past.

At the same time it would be unjust to imply that Strachey's influence on the art of biography had been wholly unfortunate. The attraction and popularity of his method obviously encouraged writers such as Philip Guedalla (1889-1945) to leave the paths of the academic historians and to write with a great liveliness in detail. He exploited a visual quality which, while present in Carlyle and Macaulay, had been conspicuously absent in the work of the more ponderous and academic historians of the previous generation. *Palmerston* (1926), *The Duke* (1931), a study of Wellington, and *The Hundred Years* (1936) all possessed these qualities though at times it was felt that they were employed excessively. He had not the meticulous artistry of Strachey and seemed unable to censor his own wit, and a verbal exuberance sometimes overflows in his work, in contrast to the control which Strachey rigorously maintained.

While Strachey's influence affected the writing of biography, and indeed the whole art of historical narrative, other influences were contributing to make the period a memorable one in these types of prose. A number of historians and biographers were making an encouraging attempt to render history readable once again. The professional historians, following Bury's precepts, had established their study as a serious discipline capable of scientific method. But they had unfortunately not achieved this without some loss of the art which would render their narratives attractive. Already before 1914 there had been attempts to re-establish a grace and design in historical writing and in biography. Hilaire Belloc's extensive performance in prose had converged from time to time into some notable historical writing in which independence of judgement had combined with great verbal vigour. A long career which had included *Danton* as early as 1899 and *Robespierre* in 1901 had continued to *Wolsey* (1930) and *Cromwell* (1933), incorporating on the way *A History of England*.

A companion in verbal brilliance was Belloc's contemporary G. K. Chesterton. His equipment as an historian was less than Belloc's, but he had great qualities of interpretation, and moments which were akin to illumination. The professional historian may find less of interest than the general reader in *A Short History of England* (1917). In biography, written with great vigour and understanding, and with what may be described as a sympathetic brilliance, Chesterton achieved such volumes as *Browning* (1903), and *Dickens* (1906), while he also composed a more comprehensive work in *The Victorian Age of Literature* (1913).

Influences such as these had shown the possibility of appealing to the general reader with historical writing, and an encouraging sign was that a number of professional historians were led to follow in the tradition of making themselves once again pleasingly intelligible. G. M. Trevelyan re-examined the whole conception of history as an art and himself supported precept with example in a series of volumes, the most popular of which was the *History of England* (1926), and the most elaborate, a group of studies opening with *Blenheim* (1930). These he followed in 1944 with *A Social History of England*, which appealed so widely that over a quarter of a million copies were sold, and thus a volume of historical writing became the most popular literary work of the whole period.

A younger writer, Arthur Bryant, had discovered a very wide audience with a volume on *Charles II* (1931), and had contrived to be entertaining without any loss of integrity in his scholarship. Later he wrote an elaborate study of *Pepys*, beginning in 1935 with a volume entitled *The Years of Peril*. This presents the story in great detail and captivates the reader by the deliberate but genuine attractiveness of the narrative. The more purely academic historians themselves answered the challenge which writing such as that by Bryant had created. Further, they were reawakened to their duty of interpreting to a wider audience the specialist studies which they had been so long accumulating. An outstanding success was gained by J. E. Neale with *Queen Elizabeth*, and a little later R. W. Chambers published a life of *Sir Thomas More*, which though original and profound and never dodging the craggy parts of the theme was written with style and a sense of design that made it acceptable to an audience of general readers.

It can be justly asserted that the range and quality of historical writing in the period constituted one of its most happy features. There were studies such as John Buchan's (later Lord Tweedsmuir) *Montrose* (1928), *Julius Caesar* (1932), and *Oliver Cromwell* (1934), while Harold Nicolson not only contributed such volumes as *Lord Carnock* (1931), and *Curzon, The Last Phase* (1934), but summarized the new tendencies in the art of biography in *The Development of English Biography* (1928).

There was always an enhanced literary quality in the writing of the social historians and the economists. J. M. Keynes (later

Lord Keynes, 1883-1946) conducted economic controversy with a great elegance of style, and moved easily into more purely literary themes in *Essays in Persuasion* (1931), and *Essays in Biography* (1933).   Among many social historians the new sympathies of the age in history were shown in volumes such as Mr. and Mrs. J. L. Hammond's *The Town Labourer* (1917), and *The Skilled Labourer* (1919).   A volume in which history and theory combine with great originality of thought and skill in presentation was R. H. Tawney's *Religion and The Rise of Capitalism* (1926).

This very brief survey of the historical and biographical writing does suggest that there was maintained throughout a great liveliness and curiosity about the past.   Particularly in the period which can be roughly dated 1924-33, there was some resurgence of hope in Europe and with it the publication of many studies which showed strong social sympathies, or some robust and confident interest in human character.   The greatest imaginative writers may feel that their period is a tragic one, but despite this the curiosity of the mind continues, and in these middle years reaches an achievement which is undistressed by the present destiny of mankind and not unhopeful for the future.   In biography, as in other forms of literature, talent and genius are separated by their contrasted awareness of the probable future of mankind.   In biography and history the men of talent make a positive contribution which profited the minds of their contemporaries.

CHAPTER IX

W. B. YEATS

WHILE historical and biographical writing developed and matured, the creative writer, exploring more profoundly the crisis of his time, found himself faced with a dilemma. He had reached an absence of belief in Western civilization, and even more profoundly a distrust of the whole future of man. This attitude had found elaborate philosophical expression in such a work as Spengler's *Untergang des Abendlandes* which was translated into English as *The Decline of the West* in 1926. The mood had been expressed with great force by Paul Valéry in *Variété*: 'l'Hamlet européen regarde des millions de spectres'. The philosophical presentation never gains full force in England, but a number of imaginative artists reach a position in which society appears completely disintegrated, nor have they any positive faith to poise against these destructive elements. It is the major imaginative writers who are thus aware of a world breaking up around them, and in their own several ways they seek some myth with which to express the unprecedented crisis of their time, and some seek also a way in which they can effect a solution.

The most impressive synthesis in the whole period is that W. B. Yeats, T. S. Eliot, and James Joyce, working independently, all find the same problem, though their resolution of it differs widely. T. S. Eliot in *The Waste Land* (1922), James Joyce in *Ulysses* (1922), and W. B. Yeats in such volumes as *The Wild Swans at Coole* (1919), *Michael Robartes and the Dancer* (1921), *The Tower* (1928), and *The Winding Stair* (1933), are all trying to discover some formula through which the fragmentation of modern experience can be expressed.

W. B. Yeats had an early encounter with this problem. He was aware philosophically of its existence before the pressure of the period after 1918 had made it apparent as a part of common experience. Nor was Yeats affected in the same ways as English poets by the war of 1914-18. For him the year of major crisis was that of the Irish rebellion of 1916, and later the war in Ireland which concluded with the Treaty of 1922. Yet the tragedy of those events and even the loss of friends in Ireland left him with an enviable serenity. In his autobiography he has himself expressed the way in which out of the scepticism and materialism of his youth he had built up a new faith : 'I am very religious, and deprived by Huxley and Tyndall, whom I detested, of the simple-minded religion of my childhood, I had made a new religion almost an infallible church out of poetic tradition : a fardel of stories, and of personages, and of emotions inseparable from their first expression, passed on from generation to generation by poets and painters with some help from philosophers and theologians. I wished for a world where I could discover this tradition perpetually, and not in pictures and poems only, but in tiles round the chimney-piece and in the hangings that keep out the draught. I had even created a dogma. Because those imaginary people are created out of the deepest instinct of man, to be his measure and norm. Whatever I can imagine those mouths speaking may be the nearest I can go to truth.' The respect for tradition, the determination to enjoy all that the Church had produced in architecture, in music and in legend is strong with him : 'At Oxford', he wrote, 'I went constantly to All Souls' Chapel, though never at service time, and parts of *A Vision* were thought out there. In Dublin I went to St. Patrick's and sat there, but it was far off : and once I remember saying to a friend as we came out of Saint Ambrogio at Milan, " That is my tradition and I will let no priest rob me." ' [1]

Such an affirmation suggests that Christendom is a larger

[1] *A Vision*, 1937.

tradition than any priesthood can maintain, and to that extent it is hopeful. At the same time all that Yeats has written here, though obviously valid for his own experience, seems too nebulous and fragile to sustain the burden of reinterpreting civilization to a world that has completely lost direction. If civilization is actually in disruption then ' the fardel of stories and of personages and emotions ' seems a rather thin equipment for the poet. It is almost as if Yeats, despairing of the world, had retired into the narrow confines of a self-consoling aestheticism. Yet this is far from the truth. Yeats had begun in an aesthetic tradition, and speaking of his youth he wrote : ' I was in all things Pre-Raphaelite.' His verses in those early periods had grace and melody, a singularly smooth and quiescent beauty. In contrast the poems of the period under review are bare and unrhetorical, but the skill and experience of the poet has made his lines most profoundly evocative. Somehow he has succeeded in maintaining beauty while yet suggesting that beauty lives precariously in an uneasy world. Further, his description of his procedure is an accurate one, for experiences, and incidents, possessions and people are transmuted in his poetry into moments of loveliness.

He seemed throughout very conscious of what he was doing, nor does he regret the past, as he moves forward into a harsher world. He knew that the melody and grace of a poem such as *The Lake Isle of Innisfree* had been heard too often, and were associated with that Pre-Raphaelite world in which his youth had been passed. Now in a new world, harder and more severe, he rejected the old measures which had been imitated so often that their freshness had been lost :

> But the fools caught it,
> Wore it in the world's eyes
> As though they'd wrought it.
> Song, let them take it,
> For there's more enterprise
> In walking naked.

He wrote this new poetry because he had to, although knowing that it was his early work that was most popular. In February 1921 the royalties for his volume of *Poems* (1895) were more than double those that he had received in any previous year.

What Yeats achieved was unique in his generation. Deprived of the traditional mythology of Catholicism he had gathered his own symbols and fashioned them into a world of the imagination. One must apply to him his own comment on Blake that 'had he been a Catholic of Dante's time he would have been well content with Mary and the angels'. The strange thing is that Yeats is able, out of his own reading and experience, to discover images adequate for the strange, compelling beauty of the later poems. It may have been that in the Ireland which he knew in his earlier days something of the Middle Ages lingered on, so that there was around him a world in which magic, mythology, and the imagination could flourish. He himself seems to have felt this when he said that the 'hurried and successful nations' had lost vision and that their poets 'see the world with preoccupied minds'. Despite his long residence in England it was Ireland alone that gave him the spiritual background for his art.[1]

Unlike some of his contemporaries he was never made fretful by the frustrations of metaphysical or theological speculation. He seemed endowed with a capacity for what might be described as a secular mysticism. If he does not interpret experience in the terms of ultimate verities, he at least removes from it the dead weight of materialism and of agnostic despair. The tradition in which he lived was untouched by Puritanism, and unaffected by commerce. It had retained a natural belief in the sacredness of the earth. In Yeats himself it is not always easy to discover where belief in the usual sense of the word ended, and make-believe begins. At times he seems to accept

[1] See *W. B. Yeats* (1942), by Joseph Hone.

magical and allegedly supernatural phenomena with a readiness
which in the realistic world would be labelled as superstitious.
Whatever the logician or the theologian may think of his
practice, it was one which kept his imagination alive in a
world where mechanism and mass regimentation were claim-
ing an increasingly dominant place. Above all he refused
to allow life to dwindle into a series of habitual reactions.
For him each new experience has a unique freshness
and liveliness. Even in a tragic world he is thus able to live
in experience, and survive, and so his imagination grows
stronger.

To judge thus is to attach less importance than Yeats would
himself have done to experiences of a super-normal character
which he ascribes to himself and his wife from the year 1918
onwards. They are recorded in *A Vision*, first published in
1925, and as Yeats realized, this of all his works is the one
most difficult for his admirers to appreciate. He asserts that
the gain ' in self-possession and power ', evidenced by *The
Tower* and *The Winding Stair*, came from communications
given to his wife first by automatic writing, and secondly in her
sleep. The whole matter is related in minute circumstantial
detail : ' A chance word spoken before she fell asleep would
sometimes start a dream that broke in upon the communications, as if from below, to trouble or overwhelm, as when she
dreamed she was a cat lapping milk or a cat curled up asleep
and therefore dumb. The cat returned night after night, and
once when I tried to drive it away by making the sound one
makes when playing at being a dog to amuse a child, she awoke
trembling, and the shock was so violent that I never dared
repeat it.'

The records of these communications include a complete
system of analysing human life and distinguishing different
temperaments, through twenty-eight typical incarnations, along
with a chart for the division of civilization into different eras.
The symbols seem often arbitrary, though much of the writing

G

is beautiful, and wisdom seems scattered through the discourses even when much in them remains fantastic and unintelligible. It profits little to question here Yeats's own strange statements on these visions. They seem, though he would have denied this, like some extension of his own deep study in Blake's 'confused Prophetic Books', and Swedenborg and Boehme and Cabalistic imagery. What is more important than the visions themselves is that from these communications, and from Yeats's own thoughts about them, there came a mental excitement which led him to read and contemplate and create with an energy which he had not known since he was a boy.

Some of the wisest things about his experiences and their consequences he has written himself in prefatory notes. He remarked that 'some, perhaps all, of those readers I most value, those who have read me many years, will be repelled by what must seem an arbitrary, harsh, difficult symbolism'. A little later he adds : 'Muses resemble women who creep out at night and give themselves to unknown sailors and return to talk of Chinese porcelain—porcelain is best made, a Japanese critic has said, where the conditions of life are hard—or of the Ninth Symphony—virginity renews itself like the moon—except that the Muses sometimes form in those low haunts their most lasting attachments.'

Those who have read Blake's Prophetic Books will recall how after a passage of rhetorical declaration there follows with all the clear energy of the creative mind at its most alert, the lines of 'Jerusalem'. So it is here, following the diagram of the 'historical cones' and preluding the study of the era 2000 B.C. to A.D. 1 which begins by imaging that 'the annunciation that founded Greece as made to Leda, remembering that they showed in a Spartan temple, strung up to the roof as a holy relic, an unhatched egg of hers', in the middle of all these arbitrary communications and visions there stands the sonnet of *Leda*, a poem strong in a dark and fierce imagination, strangely beautiful, and yet terrifying. It is a poem all compact of imagination, unlike any other poem in Yeats himself, or indeed any other poem in the language. If this is what is brought back from the excursions in these strange visionary territories it would be unwise for those who delight in verses to question that world even if they do not understand it.

He alone among the writers of his time succeeded in retaining the respect of his contemporaries from the oldest to the youngest. He had revised his own early verses, rejecting the romanticism which had grown so unpopular, and this he did from some inner need, not at the compulsive call of any changing fashion. But he did not disdain the past, nor did he enter with his new verse into a world of obscurities. Indeed the later verse is at times audaciously simple, as only a grand tried master of the profession would have dared to attempt. He welcomed the young and the new ways of poetry, some thought too uncritically. His anthology, *The Oxford Book of Modern Verse (1892-1935)*, is very generous in its selection from the younger poetic innovators. It was as if he were making a deliberate answer to the romantic taste which had dominated Sir Arthur Quiller-Couch's *Oxford Book of English Verse (1250-1900)*. Of his own verse he excluded all that he had written before his fortieth year. Some of this enthusiasm was excessive and partisan, but it was part of his zest for a living spirit in poetry, the same mood which led him to be sympathetic with Ezra Pound and Joyce. He understood, too, the great influence that Eliot was having on the younger generation.

It may be that his life in Ireland, particularly in the years of the ' troubles ', had taught him that an artist cannot be the master of a nation's destiny. ' We are the unacknowledged legislators of the world,' Shelley had said, but Yeats had seen murder walking the streets, assassination, and the death of friends, knowing all the time that the poet by his own will could not end the action, or discover the solution. But even in the house of tragedy the poet could see that beauty too walked, and that comeliness had her heritage. So this great voice spoke on, in prose and verse, and unlike most poets the strength grows greater as Yeats himself becomes older.

CHAPTER X

T. S. ELIOT

YEATS'S solution of the artist's dilemma in the post-war period is unique. As a result he creates beauty without stating, or fully sharing, the problem of his age as writers in England have seen it. It was T. S. Eliot, an American lodged in Europe and finally naturalized as an Englishman, who was to make the clearest statement in terms of pure imagination of the crisis of Western Europe as it appeared to the most sensitive and cultivated minds. As a result *The Waste Land* (1922) must be regarded as one of the most significant poems of the whole period; and it is certainly one of the most fully discussed. Eliot himself has commanded a literary authority possessed by no one since the days of Samuel Johnson, and his work has been criticized in great detail within a few years of its first publication.

Eliot was unable to accept the civilization in which he found himself. He was aware of an upheaval in the nature of man and that left him fretful and distressed. One of the influences which worked upon his original mind was that of T. E. Hulme (1883-1917), who gave the clearest definition to this dissatisfaction with the contemporary condition of man. Hulme's essays and fragments are few and were edited as *Speculations* by Herbert Read in 1924.

At first the volume made slow progress, though a second edition was called for in 1936. Whatever the number of Hulme's readers he had a profound influence on some of the most original minds of his generation. Like Irving Babbitt in America, he was engaged on an attack on the whole basis of Romanticism. He saw in the humanism of the Renaissance a movement which had placed man rather than God in the centre of things. Beginning with this fallacy humanism had ignored the element of evil in man's nature, and through Rousseau had accepted the dangerous and erroneous argument that man was, by nature, good: 'Here is the root of all Romanticism,' he wrote in *Speculations*, 'that man, the individual, is an infinite reservoir of possibilities.' All the evil rests in society, in the conditions which surround man, and if these can be removed man's natural qualities will emerge and there will be progress. One can define the classical quite clearly as the opposite of this. 'Man is an extraordinary fixed and limited animal whose nature is absolutely constant. It is only by tradition and organization that anything decent can be got out of him.' From this basis Hulme made an attack on the whole of romanticism. Even the best of the romantic poets, he alleged, had elements of corruption within them.

The anomaly is that though Hulme advocates tradition he does not interpret this as meaning the study of the great masters of thought and style. From him came the impulse for the development of imagist poetry, a movement developed in England by F. S. Flint and Richard Aldington, and in American by Ezra Pound, H. D. (Hilda Doolittle), and Amy Lowell. Hulme himself was not a poet though five pieces, thirty-three lines in all, have been published. They have a theoretical value, but seem rather the product of an acute intellect than of a natural imagination. After a number of earlier publications an *Imagist Anthology* was published in 1930. Deriving in part from Remy de Gourment's *Problème du Style* these writers elevated the 'word'. 'Poetry is no more nor less than a mosaic of words,' Hulme wrote, 'so great exactness is required for each one.'

Though Eliot was never part of the imagist movement he was influenced by Hulme's theory of the word and by Ezra Pound's practice as a poet. Above all, he accepted that strange

combination of a praise of tradition with a contemptuous attack
on the past which was present in Hulme's writings. This
enters as a powerful motive into his poetry, and in his prose
it is found as a harsh and marring element among much that
is sincere and ingenious in his criticism. So in his comment
on Meredith he writes : 'beyond a few acute and pertly
expressed observations of human nature ' he had ' only a rather
cheap and shallow " philosophy of life " to offer '. Unfortunately this arrogance towards the past, and this contempt of
writers who had been widely esteemed, attracted a number
of younger writers who were under Eliot's influence and they
proceeded to imitate him. So F. R. Leavis, who brought many
gifts to his criticism, detracts from the value of his interesting
work with numerous offensive condemnations of which the
following, again a note on Meredith, is typical : ' If any one
should comment that I have taken no account of him, I can
only say that *Modern Love* seems to me the flashy product of
unusual but vulgar cleverness working upon cheap emotion :
it could serve later poets, if at all, only as a warning.' Into
such unfortunate paths had Hulme's strangely iconoclastic
advocacy of tradition led a number of writers.

Eliot's earliest volume of poems was *Prufrock and Other
Observations* (1917). It had an originality both in technique
and in its point of view, all the more remarkable when it is
recalled that the earliest of the poems were written in 1908
or 1909. Eliot has himself stated that technically he was
influenced by Laforgue, and by the later Elizabethans, and by
Jacobean drama. To these can be added his study of the
language and imagery of the metaphysical poets, and the
influences he derived from Ezra Pound, and the attack on
romanticism and humanism of Irving Babbitt and T. E.
Hulme.

He has confessed that he was antagonized by the cheerfulness and optimism of the nineteenth century, and that he saw
art not as a means of discovering the beautiful, but of elucidat-

ing the grimmer elements which seemed most fundamental in life. He felt that romantic poetry had too often been a rural self-indulgence that ignored the realities cf urban civilization. This early volume has undoubtedly had a prestige beyond anything which the quality of the verse warrants. The effects in many of the poems is merely one of romantic nostalgia. It is as if some modern Byron in an urban and bourgeois setting were expressing his dissatisfaction with life :

> The winter evening settles down
> With smell of steaks in passageways.
> Six o'clock.
> The burnt-out ends of smoky days.
> And now a gusty shower wraps
> The grimy scraps
> Of withered leaves about your feet,
> And newspapers from vacant lots.

The contrast was being continually drawn between the magnificent gestures which life was alleged to possess in the past and the dreary emptiness of contemporary experience :

> I have heard the mermaids singing, each to each.
> I do not think that they will sing to me.

The mood of these poems was acceptable to a generation which in the early twenties had suffered disillusionment, and faced the future without any heroic expectations. Possibly the volume was all the more acceptable because it achieved these effects without any direct reference to the war. Though independently reached, it had an identity with the mood discovered in Lytton Strachey's *Eminent Victorians*, with this difference, that while Strachey consoles himself by denuding the past of its greatness, Eliot seems content to concede that magnificence may once have existed. Strachey finds a cynical consolation in proving that the past was as inadequate and odd as the present, while for Eliot there remains an unhappy contrast between the spiritual sordidness of the present and the heroic moods which once existed. They coincide in a conviction that the present is stale and drab: 'No! I am not Prince Hamlet, nor was meant to be.'

The volume, despite the almost cynical negation of its central motive, had qualities foreshadowing the poetry which was to follow. Eliot showed that he already possessed a sensitive ear, and that he could discover rhythms from the material of ordinary speech. He had an imagination, which though it derived from the metaphysical poets, was highly individualized, and so consistent that it seemed to create a world of its own. Further, his mind was already piercing beyond surface values and appearances to the ultimate basis of things.

> The memory throws up high and dry
> A crowd of twisted things;
> A twisted branch upon the beach,
> Eaten smooth, and polished
> As if the world gave up
> The secret of its skeleton,
> Stiff and white.

Thus the poet of *The Waste Land* (1922) was present in the earlier volume, though no one could have foreseen the enhanced power which the later poem would possess. Whatever may be the judgement of posterity, for those who lived in the inter-war period *The Waste Land* will remain a symbolic and representative poem. In a work of little more than four hundred lines Eliot has given a vision of the disruption of civilization. He has eliminated realism and narrative in this attempt, but instead has made, as it were, one extended metaphor, prefiguring the world's decay. The poem presented numerous difficulties to readers who encountered it for the first time. Especially was it troublesome for those who were over-anxious exactly to define the meaning of its lines. Still then some poetic unity stood revealed within it, even before the mind had grappled with the problem of intelligibility. Eliot himself, recognizing the obscurity, had appended a number of notes, though often these seem not to deal with the most severe complexities. The reader is at least soon satisfied that the difficulties have not been deliberately cultivated by the poet, but that they are a result of a profound effort to find an ' objective correlative ' for a vision of the modern world.

As Eliot stated, the title, the plan and a good deal of the incidental symbolism of the poem were suggested by Miss Jessie L. Weston's book on the Grail legend, *From Ritual to Romance*. To this Eliot admitted a more general debt to Frazer's *The Golden Bough*. Throughout he uses the symbol of the contrast of drought, and parched lands, with rain and floods. In the same way as in the fertilization myths they are employed to indicate death and re-birth.

> Here is no water but only rock.
> Rock and no water and the sandy road.

In a poem where the method by which unity has been achieved is difficult to discover, the figure who recurs most frequently, though in changing guise, is Tiresias. As Eliot himself comments, Tiresias, although a mere spectator and not indeed a ' character ', is yet the most important personage in the poem uniting all the rest. What Tiresias sees is, in fact, the substance of the poem. The characters and the sexes fade into one another and unite in him :

> I Tiresias, though blind, throbbing between two lives,
> Old man with wrinkled female breasts.

It is strange that Eliot, who in his criticism had emphasized the virtues of tradition, had here mastered his poetic problem in a work of great originality which has no recognizable antecedents in English poetry. The imagery may at times be reminiscent of the metaphysicals, but the design of the poem, its great concentration, its mixture of lyrical moments of great beauty with harsher satiric elements, its continual discovery of most fascinating rhythms in phrases of ordinary speech, and perhaps supremely its capacity for vivid, direct statement in poetry, all these were highly individualized products of his own mind. The genius for direct statement in verse, based on the natural rhythms of speech, is one of Eliot's outstanding achievements in verse. It appears in the sudden, realistic scenes where such vocabulary and rhythms are audaciously used with most telling effect. The boldest and most poignant is the public-house scene with its refrain ' Hurry up, please, it's time ', and its bold and telling recall of Ophelia's 'Good night, sweet ladies ' at the close.

Of all the considerable comment which *The Waste Land* aroused the criticism which affected Eliot himself most was a footnote in I. A. Richards's *Science and Poetry* (1926). Acknowledging his debt to *The Waste Land* for a passage in his own argument, Richards wrote : ' Eliot seems to me by this poem to have performed two considerable services for this generation. He has given a perfect emotive description of a state of mind which is probably inevitable for a while to all meditative people. Secondly, by effecting a complete severance between his poetry and all beliefs, and this without any weakening of the poetry, he has realized what might otherwise have remained largely a speculative possibility, and shown the way to the only solution of these difficulties. " In the destructive element immerse. That is the way." '

The degree to which Eliot was moved by this comment is revealed in the concluding chapter entitled ' The Modern Mind ', in his critical volume *The Use of Poetry and the Use of Criticism* (1933). Richards's criticism would seem to have acted as a force impelling him to construct a positive belief as a basis for his poetry. Such a basis he accepts, Catholic and traditional and Christian, and in time it leads to plays such as *The Rock* (1934), and *Murder in the Cathedral* (1935), and to the mysticism of *The Four Quartets*.

All this may, of course, be to simplify too much. It is never easy to ascertain the motives which lead to development or change in a poet. He may not know himself. In Eliot there is at first and there remains until to-day an innate, depressed element which seeks to expose the falsity and the masquerades of life, and is aggressively determined not to be deceived by beauty. It varies in quality from lucidity and vision to something not much elevated above spiritual debility. This deep-set attitude recurs even after the period when it has been replaced as a major motive. A notable instance of this can be found in a remarkable note prefaced to the concluding number of *The Criterion*, a journal of arts which Eliot had edited until 1939. Writing after the German invasion of Czechoslovakia and with a knowledge of the consequent inevitability of war, Eliot makes his confession : ' In the present state of public affairs—which has induced in myself a depressing spirit so different from any other experience of fifty years as to be a new emotion—I no longer feel the enthusiasm necessary to make a literary review what it should be. This is not to suggest that I consider literature to be at this time, or at any time, a matter of indifference. On the contrary, I feel that it is all the more essential that authors who are not concerned with that small part of " literature " which is really creative— and seldom immediately popular—should apply themselves sedulously to their work without abatement or sacrifice of their artistic standards on any pretext whatsoever.'

This depression was from the first closely allied to a philosophical attitude. The attack on romantic humanism, which he had derived from Babbitt and T. E. Hulme, he had worked out first in literary terms. From his poetry all romantic elements had been drained, and much of the comic and satiric elements in his early poems were an attack on all the romantic poets had elevated. From this he had proceeded to a deeper concept of the inadequacy of man and the impermanence of the civilization which he had created. He seems at times to image a despair of Western civilization as it discovered itself in the thirties. From this he reaches a Christian position, though he seems to do so with some undefinable sense of resignation. Thus in *The Waste Land*, and, as I surmise, particularly after Richards's criticism, Eliot came to revalue the attack of Babbitt and Hulme in more fundamental terms. He found utterly unacceptable the romantic substitution of individual experience, and the divinations of truth that may seem to accompany it, for the strength and consistency of the Christian tradition.

With the decline of religion and the unrest in society the artist has increasingly made bolder claims to be the interpreter and at times the saviour of the community. Wordsworth, for instance, is not using poetry to interpret a common human experience as was the method of the classical poets. He is employing art in order to recreate in us the strange and highly individual experience which he has himself received. At the same time he offers that experience as a spiritual interpretation of life. Shelley had stated the claims of the poet in even more extravagant terms at the conclusion of *The Defence of Poetry*, for here the artist becomes the ' unacknowledged legislator of the world '. Matthew Arnold in many ways did not approve of Shelley, yet he suggested that in an age of declining faith poetry would replace religion, and though expressed in complicated and psychological terms, that is ultimately the conclusion of I. A. Richards.

Against all this Eliot found himself increasingly in revolt. The degree to which he explored the problem can be seen in *The Use of Poetry and the Use of Criticism*, though perhaps he never stated it in terms which fully satisfied him. There he comments on the increasing self-consciousness of the artist, and quotes in support a phrase from Maritain's *Art and Scholas-*

ticism : ' Work such as Picasso's shows a fearful progress in self-consciousness on the part of painting.' He quotes from Jacques Rivière to show how the change developed : ' If in the seventeenth century Molière or Racine had been asked why he wrote, no doubt he would have been able to find out but one answer; that he wrote " for the entertainment of decent people " (*pour distraire les honnêtes gens*). It is only with the advent of Romanticism that the literary act came to be conceived as a sort of raid on the absolute and its result as a revelation.' To this he adds another phrase from Maritain : ' It is a deadly error to expect poetry to provide the supersubstantial nourishment of man.' Conclusions such as these are the outward indications of the changes of thought and experience which led Eliot to base the poetry of the middle period on Christian themes.

Whether such a poem as *The Journey of the Magi* has the originality and concentrated power of the earlier work may be questioned. It gains, most certainly, in simplicity and directness. As the poets of a younger generation discovered themselves in the Spanish Civil War, so Eliot finds himself in the Christian faith. His art has gained a purpose beyond itself, an urgency and a desire to seek an audience. He becomes conscious for the first time of an impelling necessity to be intelligible, and he has lost the ' fearful progress in self-consciousness '.

He had discovered his own talent for verse drama already in 1932—*Sweeney Agonistes* or *Fragments of an Aristophanic Drama*. Into this new-discovered medium he tried to canalize his Christian allegiances. At first in *The Rock* the motives seem too obvious, but *Murder in the Cathedral* has a quality in plot, character and verse which belong authentically to the tradition of poetic tragedy.

With the assumption of this Christian loyalty he has thinned the ranks of his adherents though he has found new followers. Among many there was a deep encouragement of spirit in finding one of his eminence devoting his undoubtedly great art to the Christian faith, and to the Anglican Church at a period when its intellectual adherents were not outstanding. It seemed possible that he might do for Anglicanism what G. K. Chesterton, G. M. Hopkins and a number of other writers had done for Roman Catholicism. On the other hand he lost, particularly among his younger adherents, many who had been attracted by the supreme concentration and originality of his early poetry. The latest phase in his work, the drama of *The Family Reunion* and the mystical poems of the *Four Quartets*, shows that as a writer he is not static. Indeed *Four Quartets* have a quality that will set them high in any estimate of his poetry. It may be doubted though whether he will again stand in that symbolical relation to a generation as he did in the late twenties and the early thirties.

CHAPTER XI

WAR AND THE WRITER

MOST of the major writers of the inter-war period, Yeats, Joyce, D. H. Lawrence, Aldous Huxley, and T. S. Eliot, had not participated in the war of 1914-18. Their work is to some extent engaged with the idea of war, but they are not as deeply affected as were the writers who had actual experience in the fighting services. For the war of 1914-18 had a profound effect not only on the economic life of man but in Western Europe at least on his whole mental and spiritual outlook. Trench warfare, as it was endured on the Western Front in the middle and later years of that war, was probably one of the grimmest and most brutalizing types of conflict which man had ever had to endure. The result affected the mood of the whole period. It can be discovered in the deeply cynical reaction against the idealism which had been preached, with appropriate slogans, during the war years. Similarly, in the inter-war period, a similarly sceptical attitude was maintained by many alert minds towards projects for international co-operation.

It could further be maintained that the spirit of man has never fully recovered from the lacerating experiences which began in the war years of 1914-18. Western civilization had lost the sense of its own permanence which had once been such a gratifying and reassuring conception. Western man seemed sometimes to have a longing for mortality and for the end of the traditions in which he had grown up. All that once seemed humane and progressive and hopeful, now became an evil and contorted shape. Something had entered in, cruel and ruthless, against which civilized man seemed helpless and resigned. Though many ignore this new vision of evil in life, it persists to gain confirmation in the years when a second world war becomes inevitable.

The phases of the war of 1914-18 itself were very closely marked by the work of successive poets. Supremely, Rupert Brooke had defined the romantic idealism of the early stages of the war. There were others with him, including such figures as Julian Grenfell. That early stage broke with the actual experience of war and the idealists were replaced by satirists and realists such as Robert Nichols and Siegfried Sassoon. Of all the poets of this group Sassoon was outstandingly the most effective, and particularly in such a volume as *Counter Attack* (1918) he gave the full bitterness of the experience of the individual soldier who neither remembered the cause for which he was fighting, nor trusted those who led him. Sassoon had grown from the Georgian calm of *The Old Huntsman* (1917) into this bitter experience of a new type of war that broke the very heart of man, and the journey was a poignant one. Though powerfully presented in his verses, he has explored all that he had endured again in greater detail in his autobiography which was continued as late as 1945 with *Siegfried's Journey*.

Sassoon's limitation, when viewed from the perspective of these later years, is that his imagination has remained fixed in the experiences of the war years of 1914-18. Nothing has happened later that could be admitted into the intimate places of his mind, and indeed so absolute was the fixation that later events were not permitted to intrude even if they would have helped to interpret the war crisis which he was attempting to elucidate. This is particularly notable in the autobiography where sometimes he seems to write as if nothing of importance had happened since 1918.

Fortunately the poetry of the war did not end with the mood of Sassoon. There emerged in Wilfred Owen (1893-1918) a poet who, though influenced by Sassoon's bitter poems,

H

possessed himself of some visionary quality through which the cruelty and piteousness of war were at once apparent. Owen, who was killed exactly a week before the Armistice of 1918, had shown the horror of trench warfare in his letters by an almost apocalyptic vision: 'They want to call No Man's Land "England" because we keep supremacy there. It is like the eternal place of gnashing of teeth : the Slough of Despond could be contained in one of its crater-holes, the fires of Sodom and Gomorrah could not light a candle to it—to find the way to Babylon the Fallen. It is pock-marked like a body of foulest disease and its odour is the breath of cancer.' All the horror of war is present to his imagination, though its conclusion is ultimately not satire but poignancy. In a note on his intentions, Wilfred Owen wrote :

> My subject is War and the pity of War.
> The Poetry is in the pity.

That is the theme of the remarkable visionary poem, *Strange Meeting*, in which he recounts the conversation in Hell of two soldiers, one of whom has killed the other.

> '. . . Strange friend,' I said, 'here is no cause to mourn.'
> 'None,' said the other, 'save the undone years,
> The hopelessness. Whatever hope is yours
> Was my life also; I went hunting wild
> After the wildest beauty in the world.'

The presentation of the war in fiction bears some resemblance to the values of the poets, though chronologically the fictional presentation comes later. In part this is a practical matter, for while a poet may write a brief lyric in a trench, or at the base, or on leave, carrying it if necessary for days in his memory, the novelist must have leisure to exercise his craft. Apart from this there seemed a conspiracy of silence about the war as a theme for fiction in the years which immediately followed 1918.

The smaller audience which read Sassoon or Owen was prepared to endure again the full tragedy in imaginative retrospect, but the larger audience of fiction demanded in those years immediately after the war any theme rather than that of the conflict itself and its horrors. *Rough Justice*, a commendable war novel by A. E. Montague, gained little attention because it was published too early for the general public to feel ready to face the realistic presentation of war in fiction.

The first reaction of the public after the war was to be found in a desire to forget the evil and brutality in reassuring itself that life was more kindly than these four hideous years had suggested. The phenomenal success of A. S. M. Hutchinson's *If Winter Comes*, which no student of popular taste can afford to neglect, depends on that impulse. It was the same desire among ordinary men to regain the illusion that they were civilized that gave such easy acceptance to the genial comedies of A. A. Milne. There were other writers of the same type, and in them all the underlying mood was sentimental. This ignored the state of the world and the condition of human nature, yet with all its limitations it was the assertion by the common man and by the spokesmen of common men of a desire for a kindlier world, and a belief that man would be worthy of a finer life, if only his leaders and rulers would give him the chance.

There developed, a little later perhaps, an interest in the individual, and a desire to explore all that he had suffered during the war. Somehow the belief existed among ordinary men that this suffering of human individuals had been so profound that its repetition was unthinkable. At first the mind and imagination hesitated before reaching out to discover the more hideous aspects of the experience that had been endured. Attention attached itself, at this early stage, to the dead and not to the living, and there were many dead. Sir James Barrie's *Mary Rose*, and Sutton Vane's *Outward Bound*, while they do not depend directly on a war theme, both deal with the problem of individual survival. Their authors had been led to that theme by the thought of the many young men killed in the war. They were aware that many in the large audience to which they appealed had recently had to consider these questions in a sudden and poignant way.

It was in 1929, as has already been suggested, that large, popular audiences were ready for the first time to consider the realities of the war of 1914-18 as a theme for fiction. In that year Remarque's novel *All Quiet on the Western Front* was translated into English and had a very wide circulation. It is a crude and sentimental volume with a strain that is almost hysterical. Few who had served in the war would have accepted it as an adequate record of experience, and after the war of 1939 the civilian is able to approach its records in a less abashed way. But it answered some contemporary need, particularly in its plea for the individual soldier, tormented and degraded in the struggle. In drama, in this same year of 1929, R. C. Sherriff gained an outstanding success in *Journey's End*, which was a realistic picture of the personal relationship of a group of men engaged in trench warfare. Richard Aldington in *Death of a Hero*, and Ernest Hemingway in *A Farewell to Arms*, were far more genuinely realistic and authentic than Remarque, and both these works appeared in 1929. The appearance of all these works coming so closely together would seem to suggest that it was only after a decade that the public was ready to face imaginatively a war whose memory had filled it with such horror.

This phase in which the war of 1914-18 was frankly and realistically explored did not last long. By the early thirties men's minds had moved on to the scarifying prospect of a new catastrophe. Before the close of this period in which the war of 1914-18 is explored, Frederick Manning in *Her Privates We* (1930), by Private 19022, gives one of the clearest and most satisfactory English examples of the type. Manning, though less sentimental than Remarque, is making the same plea that

the soldier is an innocent being called into brutal and degrading action. ' War ', as Manning wrote, ' is waged by men, not
by beasts, or by gods. It is a peculiarly human activity.' Like
all his contemporaries he does not think of the war as an affair
of great issues between nations. The whole emphasis is on
the horror of the conflict and on the suffering of the individual
soldier.

Manning, as he says in his introduction, is giving a record of
experience on the Somme front, with an interval behind the
lines, during the latter half of the year 1916. Like all the
soldier authors of that war he saw the civilian as a protected
and ignorant creature in safety and comfort at home, who must
be shocked into a new knowledge of war's realities. ' Keep
the home fires burning ' was the sentimental plea of one war
which would have sounded a hollow mockery in the next when
the home fires burned, but in rather a different way. The dirt
and discomfort of the trenches, the long waiting, the terror and
the horror of action, these are Manning's scenes. They are all
deliberately emphasized so that the man at home may be made
to understand. It is the work of a clever and sensitive mind,
and much of the character drawing has a skill independent of
the theme. But throughout one cannot escape the impression
that Manning is attempting to frighten the reader with the
portrait of the terrifying scene : ' All the filth and ordure he
had ever heard came from between his clenched teeth;—but
his speech was thick and difficult. In a scuffle immediately
afterwards a Hun went for Minton, and Bourne got him with
his bayonet under the ribs, near the liver, and then unable to
wrench the bayonet out again, pulled the trigger and it came
away easily enough.'

If one has to summarize the effect of literature on modern life
in England, it may be advanced that despite all its sincerity the
ultimate result of this ' horror ' literature of the war of 1914-18
was an unhappy one. It bred in its readers a mood of fear,
which was negative and ineffective. The soldier was too

ready to indulge in a mixture of sentiment and hysteria in order
to revenge himself on the civilian whom he regarded as
sheltered from his dangers. The war literature of the years
1929 and 1930 prepared for the political passivism of the thirties
and its refusal in many minds to see that Europe was preparing
for a new barbarism. Yet the writers themselves must not be
condemned. They were expressing the shock which civilized
man felt when he first met modern warfare, particularly in its
most dull and degrading form of trench warfare. Since then
our sensibilities have been atrophied by a series of horrors, and
Remarque and Manning can no longer disturb or frighten us.

The portrayal of war did not end there. In the thirties,
while the memory of the horror remained and was strengthened
in many instances with expressions of pacifist convictions,
other elements intruded. T. E. Lawrence, whose experience
of war had been in the Middle East, restored once again an
element of romance and mystery, of adventure and glamour
into what had been a dreary and sordid experience. Lawrence,
it is true, suffered physically to an extreme degree, but he had a
war of movement with the excitement of strange encounters.
Above all, in the warfare which he had known, the individual
was not overlaid by the mass, nor man by mechanism. Here
was the picture of a hero riding again into Damascus, instead
of civilized man degraded and befouled standing in endless
horror in the water-logged trenches of France. Further, Lawrence could write, and could convert his unique experience in
the war into one of the great books of Arabia, in the tradition
of Doughty and Burton. It seems to complete the contrast
when one discovers him saying in his letters of some of the
poets of the Western front that they were not tough enough.
Whatever he and his companions may have endured, their
experiences have no identity with the massed hordes waiting
death in Western Europe, nor can Lawrence suppress an
element of romance, however hard he may attempt to do so,
for he carries us to his scenes; 'the sweep of the open

places, the taste of wide winds, the sunlight, and the hopes in which we worked. The morning freshness of the world-to-be intoxicated us. We were wrought up with ideas inexpressible and vaporous, but to be fought for.'

The mystery which enshrouded Lawrence's contribution to the war continued into the record of his publication of his account of the campaign. In 1926 *The Seven Pillars of Wisdom* had been issued in an edition of little over a hundred subscription copies at a cost of some £13,000. To meet this outlay Lawrence found himself compelled to issue an abbreviated edition as *The Revolt in the Desert* in 1927, and it was this volume which established his reputation with the wider public. In 1935 *The Seven Pillars of Wisdom* was itself issued in an ordinary edition and in 1938, after his death, Lawrence's remarkable collection of letters was published.

His reputation and influence increased because his popularity was not confined to those who admired his career in the war: The Left Wing writers and even the Communists found much in him that they could esteem. For them the appeal lay not so much for his share in the Arab campaign as for the later reputation gained from *The Mint*, his unpublished record of the life of an ordinary serviceman in the R.A.F. If Lawrence had pleased the romantics by his years of endurance in the Middle East, he had puzzled and delighted the proletarians by his twelve years' service in the ranks of the Air Force. A discriminating analysis, which is very largely a tribute, is to be found in the work of Ralph Fox, the Communist writer who was killed in Spain. He describes him as ' certainly among the most remarkable figures of modern England ', and he adds that ' the important thing about Lawrence is that he is the only hero whom the English ruling classes have produced in our time, a hero who in his own lifetime gathered about him all the legendary atmosphere of the hero '.

Apart altogether from his great talents as a writer T. E. Lawrence was one of the most remarkable men of his time.

Though he had become the one great hero of the war, he realized that in the modern world the individual, however brilliant, is not enough. In a letter to Robert Graves in 1935 he wrote : ' The conquest of the last element, the air, seems to me the only major task of our generation, and I have convinced myself that progress is made not by the single genius, but by the common effort. To me it is the multitude of rough transport drivers, filling all the roads of England every night, who make this the mechanical age. And it is the airmen, the mechanics, who are overcoming the air, not the Mollisons and Orlebars. The genius raids, but the common people occupy and possess.'[1]

Two further influences united in the thirties to change the attitude towards war in literature. First, was a general consciousness of the growth of Fascism and Nazidom and the knowledge that sooner or later these would have to be checked by military means. Closely related to this was the deep sympathy felt by writers everywhere for the struggle of the Republican Government in Spain during the Civil War. This sense that war was inevitable, even if not present among the masses, dominated the more imaginative minds and gave to the 'thirties a sense of restlessness and frustration. At the same time it increased the seriousness of mood as can be seen by comparing Aldous Huxley's work in the 'twenties and in the 'thirties.

The Spanish Civil War rallied intellectuals in England and elsewhere more than any event between the two wars. They wrote of the resistance of the Spanish Government in some of those romantic and idealistic terms which Rupert Brooke had used in referring to our own conflict with Germany in 1914. They had lived, many of them, without a positive creed for decades, but now, in the Spanish Government's resistance to Franco and his generals, they saw a cause for which they could stand with a positive faith. This eliminated from their minds

[1] *The Letters of T. E. Lawrence*. Ed. by David Garnett (1938).

the mood of negative fear and horror which had been left as
an emotional legacy of the war of 1914-18.

The issues involved in the Spanish War were probably more
complex than they realized, but in the main they were justified
in seeing the Spanish struggle as the preliminary encounter of
the war against Fascism. In the spirit of a new Crusade they
gave Spain their allegiance, some with their lives, and others
with their writing. They saw the situation with more sure
eyes than their rulers when they said that if the diseases of
Fascism could be checked in Spain then Europe might be saved.
If not, then Fascism might be later defeated, but only at the
cost of the destruction of European civilization. The fact that
on the whole question of the Spanish Civil War, British official
policy had to conduct itself with unexhilarating casuistry has
disguised from many minds in England the depth of the feeling
of writers not only in England but in Europe and in America.[1]
Among the English writers a number sacrificed their lives,
including men of such exceptional promise as Ralph Fox, John
Cornford, and Julian Bell.

Form had become for some modern writers a type of
neurosis, and that pathological condition the Spanish War
resolved. They had concentrated on technique because they
had no urgency of conviction, and now they felt that the theme
was more important than the technique, and at the same time
they had an urgent desire to be understood. No longer did
the author delight in the bewilderment of the audience, for he
had behind him a cause, and urgently he wished those readers
to join in on his side. The earlier cult of a complexity that
bordered on the unintelligible is referred to, in an interesting
way, in a letter which T. E. Lawrence wrote to C. Day Lewis
after the publication of Lewis's *A Hope for Poetry*. Of course
Lawrence would probably have expressed himself differently
had he known that he was writing for publication : ' Why does

---

[1] The whole matter is well summarized by John Lehmann in *New Writing in Europe* (1940).

your period stress so much those few thought-ridden poets, Donne, Vaughan, and Crashaw—not Herbert, I think . . . when you talk of poetry being as hard to read as to write you must be thinking of the metaphysical poets. They are much harder to read than in the writing, for they weren't very good philosophers or clear logicians or subtle metaphysicians. They were afraid of plain statement and feared that their real minds were foolish.'[1] It can be argued that some of these younger poets were already seeking plain statement before the Civil War became their theme. It is not less true that the choice of that theme and the urgencies associated with it increased the tendency.

The Spanish Civil War seems to touch and transfigure the work of a number of young writers in the 'thirties. So W. H. Auden writes in *Spain* one of the most direct and secure of his poems :

> The stars are dead. The animals will not look.
> We are left alone with our day, and the time is short and
> History to be defeated
> May say Alas but cannot help nor pardon.

Cecil Day Lewis took a theme of the Basque side of the war. In *The Nabara* he describes how the Basque trawlers fought the rebel cruiser *Canarias*. Throughout the poem there is a confident reliance on direct narrative and statement :

> Freedom is more than a word, more than the base coinage
> Of statesmen, the tyrant's dishonoured cheque, or the
> dreamer's mad
> Inflated currency. She is mortal, we know, and made
> In the image of simple men who have no taste for carnage
> But sooner kill and are killed than see that image betrayed.

The same clarification of form is to be found in the poems on

[1] *Collected Letters of T. E. Lawrence.* Ed. by David Garnett (1938).

Spain of Stephen Spender, Herbert Read and Louis MacNeice.

Among those who went to Spain to fight for the Republican cause there were also poets. The most impressive was the young Communist John Cornford, who was killed in Spain. He wrote with great simplicity and force. His verses, in contrast to the entangled technique and the obscurity of much of the poetry of the period, has all the directness of a ballad :

> On the last mile to Huesca,
> The last fence for our pride,
> Think so kindly, dear, that I
> Sense you at my side.

Whatever may be the complexity of the Spanish situation, the spirit that went out from England was a crusading spirit, heard then so strongly and clearly. Would it be for the last time?

CHAPTER XII

A NOTE ON THE THEATRE

THE theatre in England has been an art struggling in the middle of an industry. Further, throughout the whole of the period under review the entertainment industry itself has been subject to the activities of financial promoters. Theatres have passed from the hands of one group of speculators to another, with rents ever mounting, and with conditions produced which have made the orderly production of plays difficult, and the construction of a great theatre tradition impossible. Against these unhappy conditions certain devoted individuals have struggled with success. At the 'Old Vic' Miss Lilian Baylis continued her repertory of Shakespeare and of Opera in English, and before the end of the period she had added ballet to the achievements of her organization and had acquired a new theatre at Sadler's Wells. Not only did she bring on new artists, but she found that the leading actors and actresses were prepared to come to the Waterloo Road to play in the Shakespearian productions at the 'Old Vic'. Sir Barry Jackson, whose selfless labours at Birmingham had built up a Repertory Theatre, made raids on London with seasons of Shaw and with other new plays that constitute some of the most distinguished achievements in the period under review.

His London management from 1924 onwards was the boldest and most constructive that London enjoyed in the inter-war years. When G. W. Bishop came to describe that achievement C. B. Cochran wrote generously but with truth in a prefatory note : ' Sir Barry Jackson is England's great man of the theatre. His influence on the Drama of his time cannot be appraised too highly.'[1] Apart from all his work in Birmingham at the Repertory Theatre and in the Malvern Festival, his London seasons included *The Immortal Hour*, the opera by Rutland Boughton which drew more attention than any other serious operatic work in England in the inter-war period. He was also responsible for numerous Shaw productions of which *Back to Methuselah* in its entirety, *Caesar and Cleopatra*, *The Apple Cart* and *Too True to be Good* were the most notable.

It is a reflection on conditions in the theatre that despite a number of successes Barry Jackson's organization made a profit in one year only over the period 1922 to 1932. The losses over the whole venture were considerable. Further, as G. W. Bishop estimates, Barry Jackson was forced to collect over £75,000 for the State in Entertainment Tax while making a loss himself. The real difficulty which faced all managements of serious plays were that costs, especially rentals, were too high, and that unless audiences responded immediately, and almost filled the theatre continuously, then losses were inevitable. Shaw's comment on the fortunes of *Too True to be Good* produced under Barry Jackson's management is an illuminating reflection on conditions in the theatre. He recalled that Granville-Barker had stated that he could only make ' highbrow repertory ' pay its way if it were rent free and rate free. Then Shaw adds: ' In those days, remember, rents and salaries, and production expenses were so much lower than at present that George Alexander running the most expensive theatre of its size in London complained that he could not carry on unless his receipts were £1,000 a week. Now it happens that this is the exact figure at which *Too True* was withdrawn last Saturday. Alexander would have run the play for six months at such business, but Barry Jackson has to throw in his hand unless the receipts are £1,600.'

One of the most venturesome of all experiments in these

[1] For this and other details see *Barry Jackson and the London Theatre* (1933) by G. W. Bishop.

years was the opening of the Lyric Theatre, Hammersmith, by Sir Nigel Playfair, with some skilful encouragement from Arnold Bennett. They proved that there was in London a large audience unsatisfied by the material provided on the commercial stages, and that given the right play and adequate publicity, men and women would be prepared to make the journey out to Hammersmith. Arnold Bennett has described how bold the whole enterprise really was : ' Nigel Playfair took what might fairly have been described as the unluckiest theatre in London. It is hidden in a slum; the slum lies off a street that the West End had never heard of, and the cab fare to which from the West End is about 4s. The trains of the Metropolitan Railway shriek, grind and roar within twenty yards of the building.'[1]

The first success at the ' Lyric ' was John Drinkwater's *Abraham Lincoln* in 1919. Playfair found the play in Barry Jackson's Repertory Theatre in Birmingham and so the piece makes a link between two forward minds in the theatre of the time. For many playgoers, and for many more who did not normally go to the theatre, *Abraham Lincoln* was the first new play of any original and imaginative appeal after the end of the war. The large character of Lincoln was most admirably presented in the first production, and the range of scene and the many memories and hopes which the play seemed to touch made it a genuine experience in the theatre, so that this piece which took only £17 for its first matinée played for a full year at this unknown theatre. It had also a scarcely concealed topical reference. As Sir Nigel Playfair wrote : ' All Lincoln's speeches, his attitude towards reprisals, towards the condemned sentry—all these things contained ideas at which the general public was beginning to arrive for itself : and reflected, and indeed encouraged, the attitude which people were beginning to take up towards the Treaty of Versailles.'

[1] *The Story of the Lyric Theatre, Hammersmith* (1925), by Sir Nigel Playfair.

Drinkwater was not equally successful again : neither *Oliver Cromwell*, despite Henry Ainley's acting, nor *Robert E. Lee* had any marked success. While *Abraham Lincoln* first gave the 'Lyric' its reputation, *The Beggar's Opera* made its fortune and permitted the management to begin a number of other interesting experiments.

Apart from these experiments and adventures the regular London theatre in 1919 was devoted to spectacle and farce. London had been a 'leave' city during the war, and commercial managements had concentrated on the plays that men on leave would wish to see. They aimed at combining the maximum of colour with the minimum of thought. Outstanding in this type was the spectacle of *Chu Chin Chow* which survived the war and on 29th December 1920 created a record by being in production for two thousand consecutive performances. Similarly in 1920 *The Garden of Allah*, based on Robert Hichens's novel, was so popular at Drury Lane that the unprecedented step had to be taken of moving the traditional 'Lane' pantomime to Covent Garden. Some of the more discerning minds in the theatre tried to give to these large-scale productions both taste and theme, and such qualities were possessed by Booth Tarkington's *Monsieur Beaucaire* which was produced as a romantic operetta in 1919. More lively than the theatre in these immediate post-war years were both opera and ballet. Already in 1919 Sir Thomas Beecham was giving a season of opera in English at Covent Garden, and there were two seasons of ballet under Diaghilef at the Alhambra and the Empire. Further, there was ample evidence that the theatrical speculators were underestimating public taste by the crowded performances of music which were being given in all the available concert-halls.

The main tendencies in the regular theatre in the first decade after the war of 1914-18 can be defined with some clarity. As has already been noted many of the London theatres were occupied by farce and spectacle of a definitely 'commercial' type, proclaiming aloud that they would make no demands on the intelligence of the audiences. There was also a demand for comedy of a more sophisticated character and this need was met brilliantly in the 'twenties by Somerset Maugham. He had begun to write for the theatre as early as 1898, and between then and 1933 he had written some thirty plays. He first captured the London theatre with *Lady Frederick* in 1907 and the play ran for a whole year.[1] His success from that date had been continuous, and he entered the post-war period in 1919 with two successful pieces, *Caesar's Wife* and *Home and Beauty*, neither among the best of his plays. These were followed in 1921 with *The Circle*, which is probably the most skilful and finished of his comedies. It can claim a place with Sheridan and Wilde. A certain moral cynicism dwells in the action, but the whole theme is lightly touched. More precisely a portrait of the degenerate pleasures of the idle rich was *Our Betters* which appeared in 1923.

Had Maugham's success in the theatre come in a more sober period, he would probably have responded with a more profound type of drama for there is an ultimate seriousness in his nature. When in the passage from the 'twenties to the 'thirties the mood of the age changes, Maugham changes with it. *The Bread-winner* of 1930, though a comedy, has sardonic elements in its picture of a stockbroker who deserts his family because he is bored with their emptiness and their multifarious claims. In 1932 in *For Services Rendered* he writes a play, tragic in theme, of the cruel effects of the war on the lives of men and women, and with *Sheppey* (1933) he portrays a winner of a sweepstake ticket who tries, in a manner too literal for his family, to carry out the teaching of Jesus. Dramatically these more serious plays lacked the technical brilliance of the earlier comedies. It is in them that his greatest achievement as a

---

[1] A useful summary of Maugham's work as a dramatist is to be found in *W. Somerset Maugham*, by Richard A. Cordell (1937), but it is surprising how little has been written about this most able artist.

dramatist lies. He exposes through a medium of comedy an expensive and cynical society, so that his plays sometimes have the appearance of being restoration comedy in modern dress. His characters have never the supreme self-confidence of Congreve's characters, for these modern figures lack much of the elegance and the wit of their restoration predecessors, and they are somehow conscious that the censorious eyes of democracy are upon them. Maugham is an undoubted artist with a great gift for the theatre, though probably with less affection for the drama than for fiction. One feels that his mind moves too narrowly upon the stage, as if he were excessively aware of the alleged and superficial needs of his audience.

He was joined in the 'twenties by Noel Coward, at once an actor, playwright, librettist, and a figure so versatile that there seemed no task in the theatre which he could not perform. Further, no one in his generation was so thoroughly aware of what the whole mechanism of the modern stage could achieve. In his preface to some of Noel Coward's plays Somerset Maugham has commented on Coward's brilliant assault on the English stage : ' He knocked at the door with impatient knuckles, and then he rattled the handle, and then he burst in. After a moment's stupor the older playwrights welcomed him affably enough and retired with what dignity they could muster to the shelf which with a sprightly gesture he indicated to them as their proper place.' Coward seemed a mirror of his time, answering its moods and often interpreting them. *The Vortex*, produced at the Everyman Theatre in Hampstead in 1924, is almost a symbolic play of the decade, and, despite the ' unpleasantness ' of its theme, it has some seriousness as if it were a cocktail version of Ibsen, with much comedy added. In the years which followed he devoted himself to the consciously carefree mood which circulated so strenuously in London. He produced comedies such as *Fallen Angels* (1925) and *Easy Virtue* (1926). When the mood of the country changed in 1931 to a greater seriousness, Coward changed

I

with it, and in *Cavalcade* gave an interpretation of the British spirit which stirred a very large number of people. So he continued extending his activities successfully into the film. Within his own range he showed supreme competence and few have been able to make the theatre answer so easily or completely to their demands. It may seem ungracious to attempt an estimate of what is missing. If in addition to all these gifts Coward had possessed a mind that had a creative power of exploring character, or of defining the great human situations, he would have been one of the outstanding figures in the whole of our dramatic literature.

In contrast to the witty and cynical plays of Maugham and Coward there continued in the 'twenties a comedy which was more kindly and sentimental. It answered a great demand among audiences who were trying to reassure themselves that human nature was not as evil and cruel as it had appeared in the war years. In 1920 Sir James Barrie produced with great success *Mary Rose*. A large number of people who had lost friends and relatives in the war found consolation in this gentle exploration of the problem of the survival of the human personality. Barrie portrayed a life in which men and women were kindly and generous and, on the whole, good, and there were many who welcomed the vision even if they knew that it was a mirage. In 1920 A. A. Milne, who in many ways can be regarded as Barrie's disciple, produced *Mr. Pim Passes By* and *The Romantic Age*, and for a decade and more he found audiences who welcomed a return to kindliness and sentimentality in the theatre.

The first boom period in the post-war theatre ended in 1921. It is never easy to assign adequate reasons to these changes of taste. The financial speculation in the London theatre with soaring rents led to the unstable conditions which made sober and enduring management impossible. The production of plays on a repertory basis was unpractical, and even the steadying influence of the actor-manager was disappearing. Further,

the public itself was ready for more solid and varying fare
than the speculators were willing to believe. Usually they
were unfortunately too late in discovering that a new play of
merit had been produced and high costs led to its withdrawal
before it had discovered its audience. This at least is true, that
in a year of many failures there were some productions of
outstanding distinction. Clemence Dane came to the London
theatre with a thoughtful play, *A Bill of Divorcement*, in
which both the problems and the people were real. The play
was also marked by the outstanding performance of Meggie
Albanesi whose early death was a severe loss to the English
theatre.

This same year of 1921 marked also the return of Bernard
Shaw to the London stage. At the age of sixty-five Shaw began
a series of productions which show him at the height of his
powers as a dramatist. *Heartbreak House* in 1921, which is
Shaw's spiritual view of post-war Europe, was not unnaturally
a difficult play for audiences who were being invited in the
same season to see Maugham's *The Circle* and Milne's *The
Truth About Blayds*. In 1924 he produced *St. Joan*, and this
was immediately successful. It has remained a stock piece of
the English theatre, making the reputation of several actresses
and constituting, if not the greatest, at least the most generally
acceptable of Shaw's plays. In the same year *Back to
Methuselah*, the most ambitious achievement in his whole
theatre, came to London after a preliminary season in Birmingham. Shaw remained popular throughout the 'twenties and
the theatres in London and the provinces had a number of
revivals of his plays. In 1929 *The Apple Cart* was produced
and here he showed a genius for giving dramatic form to a
number of the fundamental political problems of the age. Even
in the 'thirties he remained the greatest figure in the English
theatre, and though his plays in that decade may fall short of
his best they remain agile theatrically and are still a trenchant
comment on the times. They included *Too True to be Good*

(1932), *The Millionairess* (1936), *Geneva* (1938), and *In Good King Charles's Golden Days* (1939).

To the drama of sober realism the public gave a less ready support than in the years before the war. John Galsworthy's *The Skin Game* was found acceptable in 1920, and during the years that followed his well-constructed plots, which were thoughtful, and yet not too difficult, attracted attention. There was a considerable body of opinion that was interested in the problem of social injustice, and Galsworthy gave it the opportunity of exploring such questions in the theatre while having at the same time the pleasure of a well-devised dramatic entertainment. *Loyalties*, produced in 1922, possibly shows him at his best, but throughout the 'twenties he was on the whole successful with audiences, and maintained his own steady level of achievement.

He was joined in the later 'twenties by John van Druten whose *Young Woodley* (1928) was a serious treatment of a schoolboy's love for his master's wife. The play started van Druten on a career of dramatic distinction, the later stages of which have unfortunately been enacted in America. Meanwhile as early as 1923 C. K. Munro had shown in *At Mrs. Beam's* that social observation and character portrayal could be combined with comedy.

In the more imaginative and poetic drama the years between the wars have little to show. From Ireland Sean O'Casey came in 1925 with *Juno and the Paycock*, to be followed in 1926 with *The Plough and the Stars*, and in 1929 with *The Silver Tassie*. He taught the London theatre that language had a range beyond realism and the phrases that imitated the clipped expressions of contemporary conversation. He was a poet although he wrote in prose, and while Dublin might be the scene, the linguistic setting was often Shakespearian. His success continued to 1942 with *Red Roses for Me*, where his gift for putting audaciously imaginative language into the mouths of ordinary people remains effective.

T. S. Eliot, who had entered the dramatic field a little uncertainly with *Sweeney Agonistes* and *The Rock*, gained with *Murder in the Cathedral* (1935) a genuine success, though with comparatively small audiences, for a play that discovered once again how verse could be used effectively on the stage. *The Family Reunion* (1938), in which classical mythology and verse were used in a modern setting, seemed a more uneven achievement, but it led many to feel that had not the war intervened Eliot might have continued and mastered the theatre for poetic drama.

W. H. Auden and Christopher Isherwood had also made a bold experiment with *Ascent of F 6* to use verse in a play that explored character, and was yet a comment of the values that underlay a troubled decade. While the success of the poets in the theatre was on a small scale, it was genuine, and that audiences could still delight in the rhythms of speech was proved by the many notable revivals of Shakespeare that are found throughout the period.

If the drama was to develop, the problem was not to achieve success in the coterie theatre, but somehow to penetrate the popular stages. In the 'thirties a number of new dramatists appeared who gave the promise of liveliness and of fresh ways of the imagination. ' James Bridie ' in 1931 produced *The Anatomist*, a moving play based on the careers of Burke and Hare, the body-snatchers. He continued with *Tobias and the Angel* in 1932, and a number of other plays including in the war years *Mr. Bolfry*, one of the most effective of all his works. He combines realism with fantasy, thought with comedy, and he can evoke emotions of tenderness and pity. He has produced a large number of plays, and though some may complain of defects of construction, it is difficult not to realize the presence of an original genius.

In 1932 J. B. Priestley entered the London theatre successfully with *Dangerous Corner*, after a version of his novel *The Good Companions* had been dramatized in 1931. Critics were at first uncertain whether Priestley had succeeded by fortunate accident, or whether he possessed some enduring dramatic talent. The years which followed were generous in their proofs : *Laburnum Grove* in 1933 was followed by *Eden End* (1934), and in 1937 by both *I Have Been Here Before* and *Time and the Conways*. Priestley's range as a dramatist was unusual. He had a very sure skill in the portrayal of dramatic types, and a very happy command of dialogue. Comedy he had too, sometimes a little obvious, but generous and lively. To all this was added in a number of the plays a rare, imaginative overtone. It was as if amid all the boldly drawn characters and the Yorkshire fun a sensitive and metaphysical mind was operating. This appeared notably in the plays which explored dramatically the concept of time, as in *Time and the Conways*. Priestley showed here and in a number of other plays a considerable command of the theatre as a technical instrument. He wrote rapidly, some would say, possibly in envy, too rapidly. At times he allowed himself to produce mere dramatic entertainments as in *When We Are Married* (1938). But it is clear from *Johnson Over Jordan* (1938) that his mind was also contemplating the use of the theatre for more ambitious and imaginative purposes. In that play, which makes use of an expressionist technique, he explores Everyman in modern life in his hopes and perplexities. He carried here as elsewhere a theme of hope and encouragement which had a valiant quality within it. The play could not be described as wholly successful, and yet it showed a mind at work which had something fresh to bring to the theatre. Further, it was a mind that was obviously still in mid-career when the second world war broke out.

As has already been noted the war of 1914-18 did not gain any immediate reflection in literature. Certainly audiences in the 'twenties would not have welcomed plays which portrayed the realities of modern warfare. Rather they looked to the theatre for colour and verbal entertainment to relieve them of the harrowing experiences through which they had passed. An exception to this can be found in the interest in personal survival, so much stronger after the war of 1914-18 than after the last war. Sir James Barrie's *Mary Rose*, to which reference has already been made, was indirectly a war play for this reason. Further, in 1923 a younger dramatist, Sutton Vane, produced at the little Everyman Theatre at Hampstead *Outward Bound*, a subtle and imaginative play on the question of survival which was so acceptable that it was successfully transferred to the Garrick Theatre. It was not until 1929 that a genuine war play was produced, and then it came from an unknown author whose work had been handed from one management to another until at last a group of enlightened and public-spirited people determined to give it a hearing. In *Journey's End*, R. C. Sherriff gave with a realism that contained something classical in its avoidance of violent action on the stage a truer picture of the minds and life of the men on the Western Front than had been achieved anywhere else in the English theatre.

When England entered once again on war with Germany on 3rd September 1939, the condition of the drama as represented by the plays produced in the West End of London was not impressive. The war brought a sudden end to all theatrical activity. All lights were extinguished, and even had audiences ventured out they would have found the theatres closed, as the authorities were fearful of crowding people together in any one place. Gradually when it appeared that the air-raids were not materializing a concession was made so that theatres could remain open until six o'clock. This was not very helpful, and so as the nights passed and still the raiders did not come, the six o'clock rule was relaxed in the West End to ten o'clock. Audiences responded and showed that given the chance they would venture out beyond the narrow area of the West End, for they went as far as the Palladium to see *The Little Dog Laughed,* and to the Westminster for a very different type of entertainment in J. B. Priestley's *Music at Night*. That was the beginning of a new period of life in the theatre which endured despite all the vicissitudes of war.

The story of the English theatre during the war is one which lies outside my present theme. This may be said by way of an addendum. The theatre was in a stronger position in 1945 when the war ended than it had been in 1939. The Entertainments Tax was in process of regulation at least as far as non-profit-making companies producing educational or partly educational plays were concerned. Through C.E.M.A. (The Council for the Encouragement of Music and the Arts), to be incorporated under Royal Charter in 1946 as the Arts Council, substantial assistance had been given to the more imaginative ventures of the British theatre. Above all, there were indications that a new and a wider audience was in process of creation.

CHAPTER XIII

THE YOUNGER GENERATION

THE literary scene in the 'thirties was marked by the appearance of a number of new names. They were young poets, who also wrote criticism and drama, and they gained almost immediate acceptance. Outstanding among them were W. H. Auden, Cecil Day Lewis, Stephen Spender, and Louis MacNeice. Seldom has a group of young writers gained such a rapid authority, or won so much comment and criticism. A number of reasons may be discovered for this success. The writers themselves, though working independently, formed a group, and it was inevitable that they called attention to one another. They were fortunate in being well introduced: Michael Roberts made an anthology *New Signatures* in 1932, and in 1933 Geoffrey Grigson, himself a poet and critic, began *New Verse*, which, though it did much else, called attention to the arrival of a young group of writers. Further, John Lehmann exercised great talents as an editor in a series of anthologies entitled *New Writing*.

All this, however, belongs only to the tactics of success. It would have been idle and meaningless had not these poets answered some need in their own generation. This, I believe, they achieved in the 'thirties in a supreme way. Their quality as poets differs, and their permanent place still depends on what they ultimately produce, but for their own contemporaries in the 'thirties they were a voice interpreting its need, voicing, if never explaining, its perplexity, and using a new colloquial, and supremely unacademic verse to figure out the phantasms of uncertainty and horror that lay ahead.

It was a generation that felt entrapped. In a desire for sympathy it stretched out its hands more frankly than its elders, anxious to feel a communal unity in society. Yet it had never mastered either the philosophical implications of that desire, nor the revolutionary action that might be necessary to make it possible. It watched the ever-increasing power of Fascism and its inroads throughout Europe, and felt its heart grow cold at the ineptness of the national policies that were designed to oppose it. It had, unfortunately, little knowledge of its own national tradition, and it turned upon the past of England and its present institutions in cheap and inept satire. Often filled with impulses that were generous, its faith was never whole, and it waited restless and critical in perplexed and irritated uncertainty :

> Here am I and here are you.
> What does it mean? what are we going to do?

The leader in the movement, both by personality and poetic talents, was W. H. Auden. He had learned much from T. S. Eliot, and through him from the metaphysical poets, and he delighted in the taut line, the compressed image and thought that was packed and elliptical. Yet from the first he declared a natural independence of the master. He had an innate talent for lyric which reasserted itself often, it would seem, almost against the poet's will. It was something of that same gift for the musical ordering of words, and the discovery of the rhythm which appear in Yeats's later refrains. He believed further that poetry was a communal activity, and though Eliot had used the movements of ordinary speech, Auden sought out more boldly for language which had the mark of the music-hall, or the Junior Common Room, or the easy and unrestrained vocabulary of the ordinary man at the bar of a public-house.

Eliot clings to learning and tradition despite his experiments, while Auden, not embarrassed by either, seems to exult in lively topicalities.

Apart from his lyrics he made several attempts at verse drama. *The Dog Beneath the Skin* (1935), a political and moral parable which has called in the help of expressionist drama and the methods and rhythms of the variety stage, is obviously an experiment. *The Ascent of F 6* (1936), which he wrote with Christopher Isherwood, though confused by a complexity of themes, has moments of satire and poignancy, considerable poetic strength, and a genuine sense of theatrical situation. To these can be added *On the Frontier*, a left-wing melodrama which again he wrote with Christopher Isherwood. Expressionism plays a large part in the technique, and the verse has rhythms which are adjusted to those whose ear for music is familiar with syncopation rather than with a classical tradition. The theme is the exposure of the international capitalist and of the nationalist fanatic. The whole is lively, though never distinguished, and the thought gives itself airs without being profound.

When all that is admirable in Auden has been assessed the reader, unless he is precisely of Auden's own decade, is likely to remain dissatisfied. It may be that success came too easily, giving him authority and prestige when Keats was still struggling with adverse criticism. While the presence of a poet is undeniable, the reader may sometimes doubt whether the mind that supports it has that grand seriousness which one might desire in one placed in such a symbolic relationship to his generation. The gaiety and mockery, the jazz and noisiness, have as their unalienable accompaniment an adolescent quality, as if something in Auden remained perpetually at the under-graduate level and had atavistic tendencies towards the Junior Common Room. The 'thirties were the years when, if England had been well served, some imaginative writer would have concentrated on the conservation of what was best in her national genius. Instead Auden, in such a work as *The Orators* (1932), brought all his satiric talents to the stale game, already over-exploited in less dangerous times by his elders, of abusing England.

As has already been suggested, the Spanish Civil War moved all the poets of this group profoundly, and Auden never wrote more seriously than in his long poem entitled *Spain*. It remains to be seen whether his long residence in America will add to his stature. The cry of 'lost leader' is too facile and too cheap to shout after him, though those in Europe, who looked to him for leadership, obviously miss him. *For the Time Being* (1945) did not markedly add to his stature, and his anthology of *Tennyson* (1946) showed a bleak mental quality.

It has been suggested that his poetry was so profoundly English that with emigration to America it would lose one of its most distinctive qualities.[1] Certainly it is difficult to see how he could retain that immediacy and those topical elements which gave his early verse its buoyancy. But Auden has, breaking through in many ways from the first, however intermittently, a genuine poetic gift, and there is no reason why it should not rediscover itself in some new way.

Cecil Day Lewis was the first of this group of poets to publish a volume of verse : his *Transitional Poem* appeared in 1929 and immediately attracted attention. He gives the appearance of having a steadier mind than Auden, with less indulgence in the spectacular. He seldom romps in verse as Auden does. The early influences to which he subjected himself were Eliot, and Manley Hopkins, though from Hopkins he derives technical features only. His early verses are in the metaphysical tradition, with a closely argued logical groundwork, and this is marked in *Transitional Poem*. Later, particularly under Auden's influence, he permits himself a freer expression

[1] *Auden and After*, by Francis Scarfe (1942).

with a vocabulary and rhythm caught from current idiom and conversation. It is ultimately as a narrative poet that he discovers himself in *A Time to Dance* (1935) and in *The Loss of the Nabara*.

Like Auden he attempted to use the activities of an industrial and urban society as the basis for his imagery, and he is seeking some new conception of the community. In 1934, in *A Hope for Poetry*, he gave one of the early critical statements of the aims of the new school. Often one has the impression of a thoughtful and sensitive spirit, romantic, and deeply appreciative of nature, who has suppressed much within himself to answer what he considers to be the need of his age. *From Feathers to Iron*, where the theme is more than usually personal, has these qualities which seem obscured when the doctrinaire elements in his verse and thought gain dominance. Of these political poems the most outspoken and successful is *The Magnetic Mountain*, which may be interpreted as a poetic statement of a quest for Communism. With all the variations of his verse technique and of his basic ideas there remains the impression of a single mind, endowed with ' high seriousness ', and with a quiet reserve of strength that promises an increase in power and maturity.

Stephen Spender has his own place in the group, a little removed from the others. He came of a distinguished Liberal family and he had to work his way out from that background to the definitely ' left wing ' position which he was to hold. Possibly his prose works, *The Destructive Element* and *Forward from Liberalism*, have an interest beyond anything which he has yet written as a poet. He has a discerning mind, with a delicate awareness, which in another age would have flourished in romantic sensibilities. In the 'thirties he cannot allow his richly sensuous awareness the luxury of such pleasures. Instead, he seeks out for the new world of social justice which to him must be based on Communism or Socialism. As he writes in *The Destructive Element*: ' Communism or Socialism in its completed form offers a just world—a world in which wealth is more equally distributed, and the grotesque accumulations of wealth by individuals is dispersed : in which nations have no interest in destroying each other in the manner of modern war, because the system of competitive trade controlled by internecine and opposed capitalist interests is abolished.' As political thinking this may seem a little naïve, but it is the result of a genuine and difficult personal struggle and readjustment.   His most ambitious poetical work, *Trial of a Judge* (1938), shows his imagination held rigidly, as in the passage now quoted, by his political faith and argument.   It loses dramatic strength as rhetoric remains supreme over imagination.

In many ways the member of this group who began most quietly but who has persisted in developing is Louis MacNeice. He has disclosed himself as a critic in *Modern Poetry: A Personal Estimate*, and here he allies himself with Auden and the others.   But he has qualities which place him a little apart, including a wider range of culture, and a more profound knowledge of the classics.   These help him a little in estimating the relative importance of the present as compared with the past.   Much in his early work is rhetorical and argumentative as if he were seeking consciously to ally himself with his generation :

> Because the velvet image,
> Because the lilting measure,
> No more convey my meaning,
> I am compelled to use
> Such words as disabuse,
> My mind of casual pleasure,
> And turn it towards a centre.

The poems in his most recent volume, *Springboard*, while they may not show much technical advance, have a wider human sympathy :

Under the surface of flux and of fear there is an
    underground movement,
Under the crust of bureaucracy, quiet behind the
    posters,
Unconscious but palpably there—the Kingdom of
    individuals.

Further, MacNeice has experimented successfully with radio
as a medium for verse and there very probably in the new age
may be found a new way for poetry to reach its public.

Whatever may happen, neither these writers nor their successors can usefully continue the tradition of poetry which was
practised with such acceptance in the 'thirties. Viewed in
retrospect, so much of it is already a period piece, conditioned
absolutely by the temper of that strange decade. As one
anonymous critic has so ably put it, ' they felt the nostalgia
of war they had never known '. They felt too the inevitability of the war that was to come. Much of their thought
may seem hollow to-day, as idle and useless as an out-of-date
time-table. The cleverness of their imagery drawn from
machinery and the implements of warfare as known in 1914-18
has lost any element of surprise at the beginning of the Atomic
Age. The inadequacy of the thought remains thus nakedly
disclosed. Only the lyrics remain. Poetry has already shown
that it is moving into other ways, and some of these writers
have moved too. There is a lesson that they may well learn
from Yeats, who discarded the ways of his early poetry to
answer the new shape of a changed age.

Printed in Great Britain by
Butler & Tanner Ltd.,
Frome and London